Good Girls Marry Doctors

South Asian American Daughters
on Obedience and Rebellion

Piyali Bhattacharya, Ed.

aunt lute books

San Francisco

Aunt Lute Books
P.O. Box 410687
San Francisco, CA 94141
www.auntlute.com

Cover design: Amy Woloszyn, Amymade Graphic Design
Cover art: "Shefali" by Jade Pilgrom
Text design: Aunt Lute Books
Senior Editor: Joan Pinkvoss
Managing Editor: Shay Brawn
Production: Maya Sisneros, Taylor Hodges, Andrea Ikeda, Erin Peterson, Katie Seifert, and Kari Simonsen

Library of Congress Cataloging-in-Publication Data

Names: Bhattacharya, Piyali, editor.
Title: Good girls marry doctors : South Asian American daughters on obedience and rebellion / edited by Piyali Bhattacharya.
Description: San Francisco, CA : Aunt Lute Books, 2016. | Includes bibliographical references and index.
Identifiers: LCCN 2016021637 (print) | LCCN 2016028759 (ebook) | ISBN 9781879960923 (alk. paper) | ISBN 9781939904195 ()
Subjects: LCSH: South Asian American women--Conduct of life. | South Asian American women--Family relationships. | South Asian Americans--Social life and customs. | South Asian Americans--Social conditions. | Daughters--United States. | Children of immigrants--United States. | Families--United States.
Classification: LCC E184.S69 G66 2016 (print) | LCC E184.S69 (ebook) | DDC 305.48914/073--dc23
LC record available at https://lccn.loc.gov/2016021637

ISBN 978-1-879960-92-3

Printed in the U.S.A. on acid-free paper

10 9 8 7 6 5 4 3 2 1

Acknowledgments

I must start by thanking all the women who have written for this anthology, and also all the women who were willing to write. My admiration and gratitude go to every woman who set fire to the fence around her heart and who invited us to peek at the beauty and the pain hiding behind the flames. Thank you for giving us the gift of your intimacy.

Thank you to all the women who told me that they needed a volume like this, that this was the book they wished they'd had. Toni Morrison said, "If there's a book you want to read, but it hasn't been written yet, then you must write it." In many ways, this anthology has been that book for us, and without your courage and strength, it wouldn't have come to fruition.

In particular, I want to thank Josephine Tsui for being an early champion of the project, and a friend who worked tirelessly to see the "Good Girls Marry Doctors" dream realized. Thank you also to Tanwi Nandini Islam and to Nayomi Munaweera, without whom I would not have found a platform from which all these voices might be heard.

To the incredibly kind and fierce women who run Aunt Lute Books and to all the women warriors who stand with them: my thanks. Joan Pinkvoss and Shay Brawn, your support and encouragement have meant the world to all of us.

Thank you to the National Endowment for the Arts for their generous support of this project.

To the members of the South Asian Women's Creative Collective (SAWCC), the Asian American Writers' Workshop (AAWW) and other organizations across the country that do this kind of work – thank you for showing me how many of us are out there, and what we can do when we come together.

I'm grateful to have had a very supportive faculty and cohort in the MFA program at the University of Wisconsin at Madison while I was completing this manuscript. Thank you for your ceaseless cheer, and also your patient reassurance.

To the faculty, deans, and staff at Bryn Mawr College, thank you for all the work you do to prove to young women that anything, anything is possible for them. To all my Bryn Mawr women, thank you for opening me, unfurling me. Thank you for all those conversations, which continue to determine the shape in which my brain winds itself around the world. Thank you for teaching me the art of friendship and also the art of bravery.

To so many friends who read early drafts and offered much-needed advice, thank you. You were my editors and professors before I had editors and professors. Special thanks to Hannah Wood and Laura Beth Davulis for their sharp editorial insights.

Chloe Krug Benjamin, my profound thanks for your endless writerly wisdom and affection. I look to you to help organize words on the page, and I look to you when words on the page are no longer enough.

Kartik Nair, you are the person who unlocks me when I've lost the key to myself. Thank you.

Toorjo Ghose and Kasturi Sen, your genuine warmth and silly-but-serious guidance can see me through anything. Thank you for all the mirth we find together.

To our uniquely lovely community in New Haven: Kasturi Gupta, Radhika Govindrajan, Jayadev Athreya, Sahana Ghosh, Martin Mattsson, Samar Al-Bulushi, and Rohit Naimpally – thank you for your unwavering faith in me and in this project. Thank you for turning Orange Street into a home. R.G. and J.A., your love and laughter have brought so much cheer into my life. Thank you for dissolving any barriers left between the word "friend" and the word "family."

To my dear family in Calcutta and Delhi – Ranjan Mukherjee, Sonali Mukherjee, Mayuri Mukherjee, Manjari Mukherjee, Kaushalya Kaul, and Urvi Puri – thank you for providing me with shelter, in more ways than one, and for cheering me on with overwhelming love.

Love and pronaams to my four grandparents, none of whom will ever hold this book in their hands, but all of whom I feel near me, even now. Heartfelt hugs to Nani (Primla Loomba), for turning into my Nani, too, and for loving me the way only Nanis can.

Deepest thanks and love to my parents-in-law, Drs. Ania Loomba and Suvir Kaul, for the inspiration you provide, for being the role models that you are. But most of all, for the tightness of your embrace, the safety of your protection, the bolstering strength of your love.

To Romi, my little brother who, unfathomably, is now called Dr. Romit Bhattacharya by other adults – thank you for being my life-long counselor and partner-in-crime. I know why your patients feel at ease in your presence. It's the way in which you gently but firmly prove to the people in your life that you are the unshakable ground they stand on, you are the safety net against which they can bounce. There are siblings, and then there are siblings, and then there's you. Thank you.

To Ma, Mrs. Sumita Bhattacharya: What to say to one's mother, one's life-giver? What I want to say cannot be contained in this space, so I will say this: thank you for your intense encouragement, even in the moments when you and Babai weren't sure what you were encouraging. Thank you for the potency of your faith in me, your faith in us. Thank you for teaching me that love multiplies the more it is given, and for demonstrating how to let love in, like warm rays of sunlight. Thank you for the gift of whimsy, and for filling our home with a magical kind of happiness and safety. Thank you for the enchantment of your strength. On the worst day of our lives, when I was crumpled, you told me: "Today, Jhumpa. You must find the joy within you today, right now, this moment. You must not let it escape, you must not lose it." I have not forgotten. Thank you for always leading by example. Thank you for your shoulders, on which I balance.

To Babai, Dr. Shishir Bhattacharya: When I first wrote these acknowledgments, we lived in a very different world. One month after I sent the final manuscript of this book to the publisher, we discovered your cancer. Even then, I did not imagine that what I had written here about my grandparents, that they would never hold this book in their hands, would apply to my father, too.

Four months. That's all the disease gave us. I will never forgive it for that. I will never forgive it for anything. Babai, waking up every morning in a world without you is a daily, knifing pain. I don't know how others before me have survived it. It often feels as though I won't.

But then I think of your ever-smiling face, your ability to make everyone in the room feel like the most important person in your eyes. I think of all the gifts you gave me, chief amongst them the gift of my life, and coming in at a close second, the gift of being able to give and receive love. Your capacity for love was unmatched. In the moments when I feel I can't go on, I look to those gifts for strength, and I honor your memory by pushing forward, as you would have wanted me to do.

Publishing this book in the wake of your physical exit from our lives has been a struggle. But I am grateful, in these instances, to be a writer. For when I need you most, you are in my fingertips, you are on these pages. You are every page.

The only words that come to me now are the same words I reached for when I held your hand as your stunning spirit left this earth. These words are not enough. Nothing is enough. But they are all I have: I love you. I love you. I love you. Thank you. Thank you. Thank you.

Finally, I thank Tariq Thachil with everything I have inside of me. Thank you for knowing what I need, even and, especially, when I don't know it myself. Thank you for your eerie ability to distill my thoughts into words and actions. Thank you for the healing power of your love. Because of you, I experience joy every single day.

For Ma
for your boundless reserves of pure love
for the tremendous beauty of your spirit and grace.

For Babai
for your intrinsic, instinctive knowledge of me
for arming me with the courage to face this work
for pouring your golden light over my life.

For you both
for your
unswerving
unflinching
unyielding
love and support.

For the women who have joined me
on the journey of this project,
and all the others who might find
some truth in these pages.

Contents

Foreword

Tarfia Faizullah

Dear Fellow South Asian American Daughters,

I just finished reading *Good Girls Marry Doctors*, and I've spent the morning crying, laughing, or reading parts of one of your essays out loud. By the time I am done, there is no part of the bewildering mechanism that I am that feels unseen.

I'm writing you from my little room off to the side of our one-room apartment in Detroit. There is a skylight pouring late morning down on me. If I look up, I can see a rectangular slice of sky, my own to watch the world through, day or night. If I look around, it's not much by others' standards: a desk, a bed, books, table lamps, small sparkling white lights; but for me, it's my whole life, the closest external metaphor of what's inside me. Your stories remind me that all I ever wanted was this: room to dream in, a window to look out from, a door to walk freely through.

Freedom: of thought, of movement, of sight.

In my parents' house growing up, there was a guest bedroom on the second floor. It was often occupied by distant family relatives who had won green cards to leave Bangladesh for the wild promise of America. They stayed with us until they were accustomed enough to the new world to strike out on their own. Your stories remind me that some kindnesses aren't obvious. That my parents might have started out their lives as husband and wife in a one-room apartment in Brooklyn, but they weren't greedy with their two-story house in the suburbs of West Texas. I can see now that they tried to teach us in all the ways that they could that you don't need much more than a room to call home. Even if they forgot that lesson themselves, struggling to keep up with the new world changing around them.

Beside that guest bedroom was a little room with a little door: the perfect size for a shy girl to read and dream in. Even when the room started to fill with bags of dismissed clothes, I would go there, lose myself in the softness of bulging trashbags, and my brain, my vibrating, whirring, clicking brain, could finally imagine and long and dream so freely. I felt safer in that tiny little room than I did anywhere else in that big house. I know each of you had a place that was the same, and that is why you are now closing the door from your children and spouses and mothers to sit at your desks and on your couches, carving out the rooms you feel safest, most powerful, with your words.

In Bangladesh, my extended family all lived for many years in community in my grandparents' compound. Each couple had their own room and bathroom, but not much else. All meals were shared around the big wooden table in the dining room. I spent many happy summers and winters there, flitting from room to room, one set of cousins to another. Even then, though, I could see the dark tensions between everyone, tensions I didn't have words for, tensions I know you also feel so helplessly responsible for.

In the stories you share, you help us see our families trying hard to support us, trying hard to understand and forgive us each time we brought to them some new foreign concept to understand: poetry, feminism, agnosticism, dating, divorce. Each of us clumsily rise to the occasion again and again, forgiving our loved ones for not understanding, for not knowing how to defend us against the eyes and mouths of prying friends or family, all of us trying to learn a language so defiant, it's a miracle we don't burn on the spot.

৯

But there are other stories, stories you carry that you dare not share with anyone. The thoughts you had when you saw what you saw and knew what it was but dared not speak it. The dreams you lost when you realized your dreams weren't anywhere in sight, replaced by the dreams of the ones who made you. I made you, they say, and you try to say, Yes, but you must teach me to make myself; over and over again you say it, in all the ways you know how, but they never seem to hear you. If only, you thought, I had some room, if only I could go somewhere to be at peace, if only I could be let out. And then you found words, and through them, freedom.

৯

There will come a day when you realize that you have been carrying with you the hurt of one word where there were two. Sorry, you learn, is related to sorrow. Whereas an apology is a speech of self-defense. When you have said to them, I'm sorry, what you meant was, Do not hurt me because you do not like what I know is true for me. You have spent your whole life apologizing to others or yourself. You have also spent your whole life writing furiously away from self-pity, towards self-strength.

৯

One day, you realized that all you need is a little room, and you never have to leave it, and you are free to come and go from it as you please. And that the little room has been inside you all along, and is made of language, which you know is both defense and prayer: apology, and the wild longing of sorrow.

৯

Thank you, Ankita, Ayesha, Fawzia, Hema, Jabeen, Jyothi, Leila, Madiha, Mathangi, Meghna, Natasha, Nayomi, Neelanjana, Phiroozeh, Rachna, Rajpreet, Roksana, Sayantani, SJ, Sona, Surya, Swati, Tanzila, Tara, and Triveni for opening your rooms to us. Thank you, Piyali, for gathering us: how beautiful to see the daylight sloping across this house, made more beautiful by its hurts and dreams, its storms, its fears, its orgasms, its dark endless nights, its laughters, the magic of your powers.

꙰

This is all to say: real talk, y'all. Real talk.

Love,

Tarfia

August 2015

Introduction

Piyali Bhattacharya

It took me eight years to compile all of the essays in this anthology into a book, and then to find this book a grant and a publisher. On the evening before I was to submit the final manuscript to the editors, I scrolled through the document one last time, dotting every *i* and crossing every *t*, feeling excited that not only was this book about to come into being, but also that it had created for me, and for many women I knew, a network, a support group, a community.

Then, once I was satisfied with the work, I dragged the document into the "trash can" of my computer, shut my laptop, and cried.

I cried for hours that day – heavy tears that bore the weight of all the tears that had come before them, tears that held in their sheen the reflection of all the women who have had the courage to share their stories on these pages.

Good Girls marry doctors, it's true, especially in the Desi[1] community. What, then, do Bad Girls do? Surely, I reasoned in that moment, Bad Girls write publicly about their parents and guardians. Bad Girls take all the sacrifices their immigrant parents made for them, all the tenderness and support their parents gave up in their homelands, all the toil it took to earn livings and build homes in North America, and twist them into perverted abuses. Bad Girls forget how deeply they have been loved, Bad Girls ignore what it took for them to get the educations they now have, Bad Girls take those fancy degrees and use them to spin spiteful tales of woe about the very people who have devoted every ounce of emotional and physical energy they had towards the Bad Girls' well-beings.

At least, that's what it often feels like to be writing essays like the ones in this volume. So many conversations I had with the people who wrote for this book ended the same way. They'd tell me, "It has been such a wonderful opportunity to write about and let go of so many of these pent-up emotions, but the truth is, I'm worried about what will happen if my parents ever read this piece." I assured them that I felt that way myself.

What we mean by that is that we're worried that our parents will see these essays in which we, their daughters, have drawn up a list of grievances about our childhoods, our adolescent-hoods, and our adulthoods, and they will assume that we have forgotten *their* side of the story. They will think that all the lessons they taught us about honor and respect meant nothing to us and that all their sacrifices and hard work to raise us in a foreign land have resulted in this: a burning at the stake of their methods and philosophies.

I wouldn't blame them for feeling this way. I can only imagine how attacked they must feel. How shamed, how hurt. Envisioning their sorrow upon reading a book like this is enough to keep most of us from wanting to publish it at all. Because, after all, we are *their* daughters. And we are, no matter what they might think, indebted to them, grateful to them, and guilty when we think about how impossible it is for us to ever repay them.

Yet, our ambivalence about their reactions to the work in this book is precisely the reason why the work needs to be done. Because in the basket they packed for us full of the ingredients necessary to have a *successful* life, they sometimes forgot to include the ingredients necessary to live a *fulfilled* life.

Success is a funny thing for us Good Girls. Most of us have been schooled by our parents and communities since we were children not only to strive for but also to desire a certain kind of life: academic rigor, followed by a well-respected job, but within a career which might allow us to stay at home and raise our children once we marry a hard-working, respectful, and high-earning Desi man. Speaking of children, we should raise ours the way we were raised: with a good understanding of the language and ethnic traditions that were handed down to us by our parents. It is on the shoulders of Good Girls to carry forward cultural legacies.

Our parents did a lot to help us prepare for this kind of success. We were brought up to believe that we were different from our peers – and that this was a very good thing. That the hours our parents spent either driving us to lessons and having us do extra multiplication table drills on weekends or working two and three jobs just so they could afford good school districts for us… that all those things would translate into both monetary and cultural success for us in the future. They gave us every break; they tried to open every door they could so we might have access to the world.

But our worlds were not and are not without struggle. No matter how much access we were given, or what our socio-economic backgrounds were, what we were often *not* given was the benefit of choice. We were raised to aspire to this dream, whether it fit our personal life-plan or not.

For many of us who have written for this volume, there came a time in our lives when obeying these rules was no longer an option. We yearned for more. We had political opinions, sexual desires, professional passions and a whole host of other cravings that didn't fit this mold. We tried as long as we could to incorporate these feelings into our Good Girl selves, but the more we let ideas into our lives, the less space there was inside that box.

And yet, the idea of rebelling was scary. We were brought up to believe that there was no bond more sacred than that between us and our parents, and that nothing could be more dishonorable than to bring the shame of disobedience on our families. After all, didn't our parents have our best interests at heart? Just as scary was what awaited us if we gave up the safety of the Good Girl mold. What other kinds of safety would we lose? How would we support ourselves? What kind of a life could we envision for ourselves in which the home we grew up in was no longer the stable anchor it used to be? Where would our area of refuge be? Without the approval of our parents, how would we pin down and draw out the maps of our bodies, our spirits?

These were terrifying questions to which there were no answers. At some point in time, each of us was on the precipice of Good Girldom, petrified of what might happen if we chose to jump off the edge. But none of these thoughts were as daunting as the thought of walking through our lives, for decades on end, in shoes that didn't fit.

We jumped.

As expected, there were consequences. In some cases, our parents were so furious that we are no longer able to have relationships with them. In others, the landing was much softer than we expected. But in most cases, we landed somewhere in the middle. Neither were we excommunicated from our families and communities, nor could we be who we wanted to be, free of judgment and constant shaming. We were often told that we had turned into Bad Girls, that we had brought indignity and pain to our families, that we were the reasons for which our parents could no longer show their faces in society. Navigating the terrain in that moment – the instant after the fall but before the dust settled; the agony of impact before the healing process began – is what many of these essays are about.

But the essays move through other landscapes, too. Many explore the fact that there were also benefits to our having taken the risk of this plunge. Down we fell, through the rabbit hole and into an alternate universe; a world full of feminists and activists and artists and nonconformists of all kinds. We were enraptured by the conversations taking place around us, enthralled at the thousands of possibilities for the road ahead.

That's when we discovered that there was one more step required if we wanted to be at peace with our new selves: we had to find our tribe. It wasn't enough to simply walk away from the safety of the known, given world of our parents. We couldn't stand out in the snow by ourselves, adamantly refusing to admit that we were cold. We needed new kinds of shelter, new forms of nourishment.

Funnily enough, I think that what our parents were trying to do all of those years was to give us exactly this kind of protection; they wanted to induct us into their tribe, which largely consists of immigrants who have spent the last several decades looking out for each other in a country that still, after so many years, is foreign to them.

Our tribe is a little different, but just as necessary, because we are often just as scared to start our lives in our new avatars as our parents were to start theirs on this continent. Before I started putting this book together, I didn't fully understand the importance of finding community in women who are like me. It was through reading these essays and connecting with these women that I started to find firm footing in a world in which the ground underneath my feet had always felt a little shaky. I fervently hoped that engaging with this work would have the same effect on the other contributors.

Shortly before the manuscript for *Good Girls Marry Doctors* was to be sent to the publisher, I met up with six women who had written for the volume, when we all happened to be in the same city at the same time. I'd been having such productive and refreshing conversations with each of them about their essays, online and over the phone, and I had already started to sense the crystalizing of a virtual community. But being in the same room as this group of formidable writers, actors, teachers, and advocates was illuminating and powerful.

In that conversation, we talked a lot about why the production of a book like this felt so impossible, not only to our parents, but also to us. We knew that for our parents, this book would represent "airing the family's dirty laundry in public." It felt like such a betrayal of everything they'd given us.

And to us, it continues to feel disrespectful. Even after all this time, even after our many collected rebellions, what our parents think still matters to us. How our parents are made to feel is still present in our consciousness.

Most importantly, on both sides, there is the torture of love. The love many of our parents have for us rivals their extreme discomfort with our choices. The love we have for them – well, we can only hope that it comes through on these pages, even alongside our exasperations.

That afternoon, the seven of us brought these confessions to the table. We stated out loud all the fears we had about publishing this volume, all the guilt we've felt in our most fraught moments of panic. The more we talked, the more we started to feel a lightness in our chests, as if some viscous mucus inside of us were dissolving.

Something took shape that day: it was the effect we had all hoped this book would have. The feeling in the room that afternoon was proof that the power of words and the exchange of ideas can, in fact, have an immense impact on people's lives. It proved that when we as readers receive these stories and steep ourselves in the struggles of communities like this one, it changes the way we carry ourselves in the world. For the women who have written for it, this book represents the breaking of a long and deep silence. It is the book we wished we'd had when we were going through our darkest moments. We know that the act of making our rebellions public may feel tragic to our parents. But we hope they understand that in doing so, we are not trying to hurt them or expose them to judgment. We are trying instead to take a positive step forward – to build a safe space for people who have been through similar experiences. Because the truth is that in most cases, those of us who purposefully moved away from the Good Girl mold did so with an intense sense of isolation. Those who had gone before us had kept quiet about their family lives, as they had been taught to do. To transgress is one thing, to talk about the transgression is another. But what might our experiences have been had those people spoken up and told us that we were not alone? That we weren't Good Girls or Bad Girls, we were just girls, and the choices we made were not good or bad, they were just our choices?

What this anthology has given us is the gift of a symphony of voices building around us, assuring us again and again that we have built our community, we have found our tribe. Silence will no longer be our soft and steady companion.

For those people who find these stories and feel close to them because they can read the experience of their own "rebellions" into these lines (no matter their gender identity, cultural, social, or any other kind of background): welcome. We're so glad to be in conversation with you. Our feminism is intersectional, our fates are intertwined.

For those who are coming to this volume trying to engage in these experiences in ways they never have before: thank you. Your friendship and allyship are valued more than you know.

And for those who read it because they have been searching for people like us, perhaps for a very long time, I hope that with this book we've let you in on a secret: everything you're feeling, we've felt it, too. You're not alone. We hear you, and we are here.

Piyali Bhattacharya
New Haven, CT
August 2016

Note

1. Desi is a term that South Asians use to refer to people or objects from the South Asian countries, which include: Afghanistan, Bangladesh, Bhutan, India, Maldives, Nepal, Pakistan, and Sri Lanka.

Good Girls Marry Doctors

The Cost of Grief

Tanzila Ahmed

The first time I walk up the sidewalk leading to the front door after my mother has died, I'm surprised. I had expected my house to be covered by gloom, but my eyes catch the bright orange nasturtium flowers lining the flowerbed in front of my parents' rundown California ranch house. How can the flowers be so bright? Don't they know what has happened? How are they able to bloom if no one is there to nurture them anymore?

I look up at the bright blue skies, the hummingbirds, and the breezy trees. It is early June, with that perfect Southern Californian weather that people wrote vinyl records about. But this – it feels like a record skipping on reality. *Oh, that's right,* I think numbly to myself. This is real life. And life goes on. It just hasn't for my mother.

෨

As I walk through the front door of my parents' house, my mind reels me into all those years of standing in my parents' doorway playing Last Touch. It was a simple game – just before leaving, you touch the person you are saying goodbye to and scream out, "last touch!" Then you run in the other direction. The other person says, "last touch" and tries to tag you back. Essentially, it was a game of tag. My mom and her sisters used to play it as children and as we grew up, we'd play it when saying good-bye to family. I can still hear my mom saying "last touch!" and laughing while pushing my aunt's shoulder.

My shoulders drop and I sigh as I stand in that threshold, tears streaming down my face. I had tried so hard to leave this house, to create a life of my own, yet even in death, Mom still pulls me into the chaos of her life. I feel as if tentacles of an octopus are grabbing at my limbs and dragging me down. I am devastated that she is gone, but inside there is also a seed of rage at the idea of being back in this house. She is still trying to find ways to not let me leave. Worst of all, she has left us alone to figure out how to take care of *him*.

ॐ

I wouldn't have called myself particularly rebellious, though as a toddler I was prone to biting other kids for playing with my toys. But to my Bangladeshi immigrant parents, I was the problem child. They had come over in the first wave of post-1965 immigration, landing in Los Angeles. Mom had agreed to an arranged marriage to a man she didn't even see before her wedding day for the chance to move to America. She was an educated and independent city woman, but Dad was from the village. Mom wanted to come to the US so that she could pursue her masters degree and a better life for her kids. So she married him – sight unseen. For the first few years of their marriage, he only allowed Mom to wear saris when they went out. She never completed her masters.

I have distinct memories of being little and Dad spinning often into a rage, grabbing the closest thing to his hand, usually a hanger or a three-foot stick he kept in the front closet. I learned young how to lock myself in the bathroom, the only room in our house with a lock. As soon as I saw the fire in his eyes, I'd race to the bathroom, slam the door, and sit with my back pressed up against the door, heaving and crying. I knew he would then go look for a bobby pin to undo the lock. And then, mightily, I'd use all my little person strength to push back on the door.

And Mom, she was never physically there to protect me – she never intervened in his rages. After each episode was over, and I'd cry into my pillow, bruised and in pain, she'd come in to rub my back, and say, "You know how he has a temper. Why did you say anything? You should have been quiet. You two are both alike, hot-headed."

Mom's role in the house became one of the neutralizer, the one to make sure that Dad and I never talked to each other. Because if we didn't talk to each other, than we couldn't get angry at each other, right?

As I grew older, I learned to hide the sticks and the bobby pins when he was out of the house. My younger sisters were born a few years after I was, but by the time they came along, his rage had started to subside. They never felt the wrath that I experienced. At thirteen, I ran away to the neighbor's house and failed because she wasn't home. In my later teen years, I was probably kicked out of the house three times – for moving his things in the garage or wearing a tank top. The things that set off these fits of rage were tame by any standard. The most rebellious things I did included attending a punk show (to which Mom drove me and waited in the car until the show was over) and going to school-sponsored dances (at which I was required to work, since I was in student government). But of course, Dad didn't know about any of that – it was our little secret, Mom's and mine. We'd tell him it was a school function and, if I wanted to get into a good college, I had to go. By the time I was eighteen, I promised myself that I was going to leave that house and never come back.

It isn't until the next morning that I finally get to see her. I'm in a mortuary. It smells terrible. It's the smell of camphor and death and water and sterility. She's lying on a metal table, under a white sheet. In Islam, it's the responsibility of the women from the local Muslim community to wash the dead in preparation for burial. But I don't want to be one of the people to wash her – I just want to see her. It has already been twenty-four hours since that devastating phone call I received in my Oakland apartment, and I still haven't seen her. Now the ladies from the mosque are hovering over her, reciting prayers and washing her methodically. They are whispering suras, folding her in white cotton.

I am scared that I'm not Muslim enough to know what to say or how to honor her in the right way. I have propelled my rebellion so far that I'm not sure I am allowed in this space anymore. My mother's sister pulls me over, closer to the body, as I shy away. "You have to wash her," she says. "See, look how peaceful she is. You'll regret it if you don't help." I look down. It looks as if she is sleeping. "Take this paper towel and dry her hair. Just do it."

Feeling the weight of Mom's head in my hands makes it all too real. I didn't know a head could feel so lifeless. It is her hair. It is her face. But it isn't. She is gone. My tears flood my face as I sob uncontrollably. But I take the paper towel and dry her hair, determined to do this right. Between sobs, I try to repeat the suras the ladies tell me to say, but I can't keep up. They see me, frustrated, and quietly the lead woman tells me, "Just say Ameen." So that's what I do. I just say Ameen. Ameen. Ameen. Ameen. The women tell me that angels swoop near death, and if you say Ameen at the same time an angel does, all sins are forgiven. So I say it, Ameen, Ameen, Ameen.

They hand me a square of a white cloth. I fold it the way she had taught me – corner to corner. I lift her head, place the cloth under it, then tuck the other corners around her neck. I tenderly push away the stray pieces of hair that are peeking out. I'm reminded of how, as a kid, I was taught that stray hairs under hijabs are sinful. So now I tuck with a gentle fierceness. Mom is going to Allah now, and I am going to send her off the way she would have wanted.

I touch her one last time. It is a few hours later, as my sisters and I sit by her for the viewing. Only women are allowed to pay their respects, except for Dad. She is wrapped completely in white cloth, from her head to her toes. I open up the cloth that covers her face so that only her eyes, nose, and mouth show. She is propped on a table, and ladies walk through as if she is a museum exhibit. Some with sadness, some with fear in their eyes, some with suras on lips. The azaan is summoning us for Friday prayer and the janaza prayer – the funeral prayer – will follow. I hyperventilate, sobbing helplessly, knowing that this is it, my "last touch" with Mom. I fold the white cloth over her face, first one side then the other. I retie the white cotton ties around her, and now they are closed.

৵

"I need to borrow some money," Mom said to me, over the phone. She said it in that authoritative tone – it wasn't a request, but a command. Something I had to do because she was my mother.

"Mom, I'm unemployed and trying to hustle for work. I don't have that much money. How much money do you need?" I asked, irritated. I had just finished working on a city council campaign for which I had moved from Los Angeles to Oakland. I had always dreamt of living in the Bay Area, and when the opportunity to move to the Bay to run a campaign came up, I jumped at the chance. In those short few months I had fallen in love with the Bay the way I knew I would – I loved the community of South Asian activists that I met while living there, and within a few months, I was active in starting a radical camp for Desi youth. I had even reconnected with a guy. I was picking up random PR gigs and had even bartered a portion of my rent for my roommate's business. My parents weren't exactly happy or understanding of my career choices, but they had relented after I got my masters degree in public policy. They could at least tell their friends I had a masters. In Oakland,

I was hustling to get by, but outside of Los Angeles, I was thriving. I was determined to make Oakland my new home.

"I need $4,000. I need to pay the property tax for the house. It's actually $7,000 total, but I have $3,000 already. I just need the rest. I'll pay you back," Mom said.

"Why can't you ask Dad for it? Isn't this the whole reason he's going to Bangladesh? To sell his property and bring back the money? And why is it so much money?" I responded, exasperated.

"Your dad can't know about this. He never knows what's going on, anyway. It will only make him upset and he doesn't know the trouble the house is in."

I sighed. Despite all the patriarchy Dad exuded, it had always been Mom that had been in charge of the finances in our house. And I knew how he could be. I barely had $8,000 in my bank account and she was asking for half of what I had. I had expenses but I knew money was tight for my parents – they were both cashiers in service industry jobs and they made just enough to get by. After some prodding, Mom revealed that the government had threatened her with a lien on the house because of missed back taxes and that was why the property tax was so high. Things were a lot worse than I had thought.

By the time I got to Los Angeles a few weeks later, my rage had festered. I sat in the living room my first night there, as Dad shared what he got from his recent visit to Bangladesh.

"Here," he handed me a velvet box with his pride evident on his face. "I bought you and your sisters gold, for your weddings."

I looked down at the box in my hand. Inside were gargantuan, gaudy gold necklaces and earrings. He had spent all of the money from the property sale on this box of so-called wedding gold. I wanted to throw all of it against the wall.

"But none of us are getting married!" I exclaimed. "We're not even close to getting married. And all three of your daughters are unemployed!" I was trying hard to keep the rage out of my voice, but I wasn't succeeding.

"I know no one is getting married," he replied gruffly. "But you can save it until then. Now you have it."

How disconnected he was from reality, I thought to myself. He didn't even know that these trinkets could have kept the house from being pulled out from under him, or how his daughter didn't want wedding gold that she was never going to use – she just wanted to make rent.

჻

As I was packing to return to Oakland, Mom walked into my childhood room. She asked me to cut her a check, so I did. Parting with the check hurt. And Mom saw it on my face. She hugged me and I held stiff. I knew it was implied that this was our secret. We packed the car and she drove me to the airport. As I pulled my bag out of the trunk, she came out of the car to give me a hug goodbye. I was upset, and stiff, unable to return the hug warmly. She grabbed my hand with hers and I felt her shove a piece of paper in it. I looked down to see a $100 bill. You have to eat, she said. Spend it on food, she said.

The symbolism wasn't lost on me. In our culture, "Did you eat?" means "I love you." I knew.

And that was our last live touch.

꙳

It is a beautiful day for a funeral. The palm trees sway gently and the sky is a piercing blue. At the Muslim graveyard, I grab my sisters' arms as we stand to the side of the hole, unsure of what the customs are. It would usually be Mom who told us what to do.

We watch and whisper prayers as a group of men unload the wrapped white body from the hearse and slowly carry it to the grave. Dad was off shaking the hands of the Important People that had showed up for the funeral – he didn't once make eye contact with the three of us, his daughters.

Without Mom here, a fierce protectiveness takes over me. I hold my sisters tight, making sure they can see everything that is happening as the men slowly lower the body into the grave and place the face towards Mecca. Dad stands on the other side of the grave and doesn't notice as the uncles try to move us back – in Islam women aren't allowed to "see." I push back. This is my Mother and we are her daughters, and we are women – it is our duty to be by her side. "We are standing right here, and we are watching," I say through gritted teeth.

The crowd parts so we can see. We watch as the men one by one drop handfuls of dirt into the hole while reciting suras. It is only after the grave is full and the men have left that my sisters and I reach down for a handful of dirt to drop in ourselves.

Mom was religious, but not in the dogmatic way Dad is. She prayed, read Quran, fasted proudly, but never pressured us to do the same. She sewed cotton prayer scarves on her Singer for the women in the community. She would make sure women were represented in their masjid-cum-office-complex that they started with the local Bangladeshi community. It was not a surprise, then, but a miracle all the same, that the last audible words my Mom uttered on this planet were, "I'm praying."

My middle sister was the last person in our family to see my mother semi-conscious. Lying in the hospital bed, Mom was moving her finger across the sky, like she was reading something. She was delirious, half alert, barely able to speak. My sister asked her, "What are you doing? Are you praying?" Mom responded, "Yes, I'm praying." And then her system crashed. They couldn't save her. She died a couple of hours later. Those were her last words. "I'm praying." How unbelievably strong must her faith have been that prayers were her last words? May my faith be even a fraction of the strength of Mom's. May Allah accept her.

I kneel down by the dirt, freshly piled. People are slowly milling away, talking about how young she was or how sad it is for the children.

"Mom," I whisper, not wanting anyone to hear me. "As soon as everyone leaves, the angels of death are going to come to you and ask you questions. When they ask, don't forget to answer: Allah is your God, Prophet Muhammad is your messenger, and you are a Muslim. Everything will be okay. Don't be scared."

At that moment, my little sisters wander over and kneel by me. I feel the fierceness of loving them so hard, remembering the days they were born, and how without Mom here, I am going to love and protect them from everything.

◈

Mom called me a couple weeks before she died. "I have the money to return to you," she said. "I'll put it in your bank account."

Our relationship had been strained ever since she'd borrowed my money. Our calls had become more infrequent, and I was cold when she did get ahold of me on the phone.

"Where did you get the money from?" I asked suspiciously.

"I have my ways!" she responded in a singsong voice.

Now, as I sort through her things, I hope I will find a clue. I know money was tight, and I still haven't figured out where she had found the money to pay me back. My sisters and I go through piles and piles of unopened bills, trying to get the finances in order. I keep a lookout for any clue as to how she could have got that extra money. It is only after going through all the bills that I realize just how much financial trouble Mom was actually in – that several bills are in the red and several more are in collections. We have to rush a payment so the electricity in the house doesn't get turned off. I can't believe it has got to this point, and that after thirty-two years of marriage, Dad still has no clue.

So we sort – drawers, saris, perfume bottles. All the sorting that comes with death. As I clean out Mom's purse, I find the compact mirror I had bought her in Paris when I was eighteen. Buried at the bottom, I find a receipt. I look close and see that is for a gold buyer, dated for just a few weeks back for the amount of $4,000. My heart starts racing, and I run to her room to rip open the jewelry boxes that she keeps hidden in the linen closet. Sure enough, one specific red velvet box from Bangladesh is empty.

I sigh heavily. In Bangladeshi culture, all a woman has is the gold jewelry given to her on her wedding day. Mom's gold jewels were some of the few things in the house that were truly hers. Gold jewelry is a Bangladeshi woman's safety net and savings – only to be used for financial emergencies. Here we were in 2011, with Dad buying his daughters (who weren't even close to getting married) wedding gold, while Mom was selling her own wedding gold to pay me back the money she had borrowed. What must she have been feeling in the moment she handed the bangles over to the pawnshop owner? Was my ability to live my life on my own worth my mother's wedding gold?

I show Dad the receipt, and once he digests what has happened, he breaks down, too. "I didn't know it was this bad," he says. "Why did she have to sell her gold? Why didn't she tell me? I would never have wasted the money on buying you guys wedding jewelry had I known…"

I'm sitting in the driver's seat as I drive Dad around on errands. My parents did not have an end-of-life plan figured out and were even more blindsided by the fact that Mom had died so young. She was only fifty-five. In the period of forty days after her death – the Muslim mourning period – I create an epic things to do list of Things to Do After Mom's Passing. As the oldest daughter, I feel that it is my duty to Mom to make sure things are okay. In addition to endless calls, these errands include a lot of driving Dad around – to the social security office, the DMV, the insurance company and doctor's offices.

These rides with Dad are awkward. It is the longest amount of time we have ever spent alone together, for as long as I can remember. I don't know how to make small talk with Dad. So much of my life has been spent trying to avoid him and his temper. His temper is gone now. Mom's death has aged him overnight and his reactions are delayed.

And there is the huge elephant in the room. How am I supposed to spend the rest of my life taking care of this man, without Mom to be my buffer? How are we going to pretend for the rest of our lives that he never abused me?

We are driving back from the accountant after asking him all of the tax questions that popped up once all the secrets Mom had been keeping were revealed. In the car, I try to make conversation. I ask a random question about how a certain Bengali uncle had met his non-Bengali wife. In his grief, Dad is prone to speaking in Muslim proverbs. He responds to my question with a proverb about forgiveness and how we must never do harm to others. The hypocrisy pushes me over the edge.

"How can you say that?" I say. "You used to hit me as a child. Don't you remember how you used to hit me?"

"I never hit you," he responds, his voice tightened. "Maybe I hit you only that one time when it was really bad. And I didn't mean to hurt you."

Tears quietly drip out of the side of my eyes as my grip on the steering wheel turns my knuckles white.

"But Abbu, you did. How could you forget? All those times I locked myself in the bathroom? Don't you remember how I ran away?"

"I don't remember! It was such a long time ago. I needed you to respect me. But please forgive me. I only remember that one time. In Islam, you have to show forgiveness. Don't hold it against me. I can't die with this hanging over me."

"I forgive you." I say it matter of factly and quietly. I try to believe the words that I've just said. But in my heart, I'm not sure if it could actually be that easy.

How do you forgive a father who doesn't remember what he did? I think to myself. I wipe the tears on the back of my hand and keep driving us home.

꧁

The sun beats down as the four of us sit cross-legged around the head of the grave. Though piled high, the dirt has receded, caked into dry, flat pieces. Unlike exactly last year at this time, the graveyard is completely empty except for the four of us sitting around the grave.

Abbu recites suras while his fingers mindlessly play with a dirt rock on the top of Mom's grave. Sura Al-Fatiha, the Kuls, a couple more. I know his repertoire of suras is limited to the short ones, just like mine. He recites them quickly and under his breath, all the while cracking dirt clods with his fingers. Once he finishes a set of suras, he starts over from the beginning. I watch him recite, his three daughters sitting to his left. Once he cracks a dirt clod, he picks up another one, slowly and methodically moving up the grave. It is slightly morbid, the crumbling of the grave dirt. But it is as if he is embedding each piece of raw dirt with prayers, creating a virtual blanket of suras to cover Mom.

I think about how complicated life is and how complicated their life together must have been. Mom had been so upset in those last few months before she died, at Abbu, at life. And I, too, had been so upset, for so much. But as we sit around that grave, I feel none of the bitterness I had before, and all the assumptions I had about us as a family not making it to this point have dissipated. There is a serenity. There is a calmness. The anger is gone. And I can tell that whatever anger Mom had is gone, too. All that is in its place is compassion and forgiveness.

Maybe that is the takeaway. This past year, I have learned to forgive and to work with compassion despite whatever anger or animosity I have felt. Life is complex. It's never black and white. It's solidly gray.

"Let's pray," Abbu says, as he looks at me standing under the shadow of the tree. I look over at my two younger sisters and my dad sitting by the grave, all with cupped hands.

I cup my hands in front of me and lift them and I pray, giving dua. When I run out of Arabic words, I repeat English words, asking for Allah to keep my mother safe, to take her to Jannah. I pray so hard. And then the wind gust comes. It comes with such an intensity that it whistles through the branches of the tree under which we're sitting, as if it is a roaring train.

Our prayers are being heard.

And maybe everything is going to be okay.

My Mother, the Rebel

Jabeen Akhtar

I expected to have a hunter's rifle pointed at my face someday.

After the newsletter arrived in my family's mailbox, the one with the article that would change my life forever, I expected to engage in activities that could very well lead to my arrest, get me kicked out of school, offend the Pakistani community, maybe even get me an FBI file with my name boldly stamped up top.

What I didn't expect was for my mother to be by my side the entire time, charging the way forward.

I was the first in my family to read it. I was thirteen the day I went outside to check the mail and found, atop a heap of bills and ads, a low-quality newsletter with a picture of a cow on the cover. The cow had big, inky eyes and the type of soft, maternal expression harkening to children's books and dairy ads with watercolor painted bovines in aprons and bonnets baking mulberry pies for their excited, spirited little calves. The newsletter cow sat on dirt with her hind legs stretched oddly perpendicular to her belly. The title asked, "The Greatest Cruelty?" It was unclear why the newsletter was sent to my family; maybe it was just a random mailing, but the title and picture piqued my interest enough to read on.

"The stockyard workers proceeded to beat and kick her in the face, ribs and back…They used the customary electric prods in her ear to try to get her out of the truck, but she still did not move. The workers then tied a rope around her head, tied the other end to a post in the ground and drove

11

the truck away. She was dragging along the floor of the truck and fell to the ground, landing with both hind legs and her pelvis broken."

She was a "downed cow," an agricultural term, I would learn from the newsletter, for a sick or injured factory farmed cow who has become immobile. And down on the ground this cow remained, urinating and defecating on herself, dragging herself along the highway in search of a clean, cool spot.

I could hardly read on but I was two paragraphs from the ending, and I was invested in this cow's story. Surely, someone would come along and euthanize her, relieve her of her pain. There were laws, after all, rules and regulations meant to protect animals like her.

She was shot, the newsletter said. Her body sold for $307.50 and added to our meat supply.

"Hey," I remember my sister shouting to me from her upstairs bedroom window. "What are you doing out there?"

It was 1987. Ronald Reagan was president. The stock market had crashed. *The Cosby Show* ruled the networks and Def Leppard's *Hysteria* ruled the airwaves. My older brother, two older sisters, and I huddled under our desks when the sirens went off outside school, learning how to protect ourselves from nuclear annihilation if the USSR struck first, knowing full-well that the only thing surviving a mushroom cloud would be the cockroach scuttling across the linoleum floor. Afterschool was spent at the Time-Out arcade where we'd marvel at the rich kid who aligned his legion of quarters across the Frogger console.

"Read this," I had told my sisters once inside, handing them the newsletter.

I went to my pink-wallpaper-covered room and shut the door. I was confused. I wanted to hit something, to beat up those people who made that cow suffer, punch them with my own fists. I wanted to scoop her into my arms and kiss her above her big, inky eyes and ask her to forgive my species for what we had done. I never realized I could feel so strongly about a cow. Cows had to do with farms, countryside, tractors, and hay bales. They had nothing to do with me and the concrete sidewalks and cassette tapes and chlorinated swimming pools that marked my suburban life.

Except they had everything to do with me. Crouched on the floor of my room surrounded by my stained and dusty stuffed animals, they were decaying in my stomach.

I eat cows and other animals, I thought. Maybe I even ate *her*.

It would be real simple, I told myself. I would just walk downstairs and tell my parents I was no longer eating meat. Not just pork like a good Muslim girl, Mom and Dad, *all animals*. And I wouldn't care if they disagreed. If they insisted I eat meat, they'd have to shove it down my throat. I would tell them that.

I wasn't used to challenging their authority. This would be a first. If my parents had ever expected me to rebel, they probably expected the usual – all the cliché things a Pakistani girl can do like sipping a rum and coke or wearing cropped shirts or letting a boy touch her thighs. Me? I was going to swear off the ignorance and comfort and brain-washing that had marked my short life. I was going to declare free agency in the form of valuing animals more than societal norms. I was going to crawl through the jungle covered in warpaint with an M16 assault rifle fixed with an underbarrel grenade launcher slung over my shoulder like Arnold Schwarzenegger in *Predator*. I was going to fight for animals. This was war and anyone standing in my way, including my parents, was my enemy.

But before I could even get suspended for putting "Meat is Murder" stickers on all the school cafeteria sandwiches, my mother appeared in my room. She stood at the door, clutching the newsletter. "No more meat in this house," she said. She told me that my sisters had agreed with the no meat declaration and she would convince my father and brother, well, maybe not my brother because he was already a lost cause, but she was no longer buying meat, cooking it, or serving it and to hell with people who treat other beings like this. Never again would we be blind to animal abuse. Things were going to change for our family.

So much for being Arnold. Rebellion just isn't as rebellious when your own mother joins you, and, as I would soon learn, is better at it than you.

The women in my family went vegetarian overnight. This was at a time when there were no veggie burgers in the freezer section of the local grocery. You drove to the health food store forty minutes out of the way and bought a dry mix pack, blended it with water, formed a patty, and fried it. There were no vegetarian celebrities, just those people loitering about after Woodstock who ate things like millet and nutritional yeast. Yet my mother, sisters, and I needed no transition period. We weren't tempted to cheat.

My older brother continued to eat McDonald's every day on the drive home from his job at McDonald's. And my father, while sympathetic to the animal rights cause and donating bigger and bigger chunks of his paychecks to support it, often thought about the Pakistani community with whom he had copious business connections. We can be as radical as we want at home, he reasoned, but outside we had an image to keep up. Animal rights fell outside the realm of issues Pakistanis were allowed to care about: Israel, AIPAC, Kashmir, and oil. We cared about pigs. Of all things! I had once asked a Pakistani girl if the Quran really said pigs were filthy or if it was just a bunch of Muslims being assholes. She said my parents were too liberal and I was trying too hard to be American. I felt for my father. I could hide from these Pakistanis but he couldn't. Can he at least eat fish at lunch meetings if it's out of the house, he asked my mother? People could say things behind his back if he doesn't … maybe even not offer him their business. He'll be compared to those long-haired types who don't bathe. Or Pakistanis will think he worships goats. "What's worse?" he demanded of my mother in one of their many heated discussions over food. "Being called a hippie or a Satanist?"

I'm sure my father felt he brought this on himself. After all, he had refused every arranged and conventional marriage prospect in his hometown to marry the nursing student from Lahore – the alluring little beauty with the caked 60's eyeliner his friends had warned him to stay away from because she was argumentative and touchy, always asserting her autonomy from men and even the head nurse at her school. She had petite arms that could forcefully rip the bandage off a patient's head in one crisp movement. She had a temper that struck like darts – indiscriminate with just enough of a prick to leave some lasting pain. She felt nothing or all-consuming passion. It was clear which direction she was taking as a result of the newsletter.

For our first big protest, my mother forced us out of bed at 5:00 AM on a misty Labor Day morning, packing my sisters and I into her station wagon and tossing in bags of trail mix. "We're protesting caged pigeons being shot," she said. We drove three hours to a heavily wooded town in Pennsylvania called Hegins. Every year, thousands of pigeons were transported to Hegins for the Fred Coleman Memorial Shoot. During this shoot, the pigeons were released from cages and immediately shot as they fluttered, disoriented, towards the sky. The pigeons who fell onto the field still alive had their throats twisted and throttled within the small, puffy hands of little boys. Some birds escaped the shooting range only to succumb to the bullet wounds that had penetrated their wings, chests, or eyes. My mother had volunteered to use her nursing skills to help save those injured birds or release them of their pain through euthanasia. My sisters and I positioned ourselves at the perimeter of the range with hundreds of sign-holding protesters and an equal number of cops.

What do we want? *Animal rights!* When do we want it? *Now!*

Hegins scared me. The townspeople weren't like the people in the suburb I grew up in. They were the type of people who ate things I didn't understand like ham hock and who the evangelists on television implied were the real Americans while the rest of us were frauds. Hegins seemed to exist in a bygone era where whites openly exerted their power over whomever they wished. I wondered if minorities lived there. My mother, sisters, and I were certainly the only brown people at the protest. Outsiders amongst the outsiders who had traveled from all over the East Coast to converge on this small town. I wondered what the rest of Hegins was like, and maybe, if I was being judgmental, my fear making me irrational. Maybe this field of mass slaughter wasn't a true representation of a town I had only been in for several hours.

My sisters and I watched as two dozen men marched past us gripping confederate flags and wearing white robes with white triangular hoods.

The KKK showed up. For what reason, other than to add to the chaos or for free media attention, no one really knew. But this was not a movie or some grainy black-and-white photo in one of my history books. I could see blue eyes peering out from the crudely scissored holes in their hoods. And right at that moment, my mother decided to emerge from the medical tent to join her daughters at the protest, which meant walking right past the men in robes. I saw a hood turn.

I froze. Something was about to happen, something bad. I felt my breaths become shallow and rapid.

"Go home wetback!"

It was loud with the protesters shouting at Hegins residents and Hegins residents shouting at us and people on both sides getting arrested. Maybe that's why my mother did what she did next – take a few steps closer to the KKK man who yelled at her. Stood just two feet away so he could hear her better.

"What the hell is a wetback?" she asked him.

Maybe he was startled or wasn't expecting a brown woman to talk back to him, in perfect English, up in his face, with a tinge of annoyance. But it seemed to shut him up, if momentarily. My mother resumed her walking until she reached my sisters and me in the protest line. I asked her if she was alright. She said no ... an injured pigeon she was trying to save went into cardiac arrest in her hands.

Her response to my question shook me to the core.

I meant, the KKK man, Mom. Are you alright after what he said to you?

It was as though the incident hadn't even registered with her. She seemed so utterly unfazed by the KKK man's presence, his personal attack towards her. My mother is barely five feet tall. She's a woman from a developing country – the world's most prized victim. She was supposed to be afraid of this big, tall white supremacist, but she wasn't. Her determination, her single-mindedness in saving pigeons regardless of the town we were in or who was threatening us, astounded me. I almost felt ashamed. I knew I was just a kid, but even if I had aged thirty years instantaneously and I was not my mother's daughter but her peer, I'd feel like a coward standing next to her. What does it take to be so brave, I wondered? Is my mother a badass, or just crazy? Or both? Whatever it was, I wanted some of it. My mother reminded me why we were in Hegins, about our battle and who our target enemies were. I looked at her empty hands, where the pigeon had been held. With compassion instead of war paint, conviction instead of an assault rifle, my mother was Arnold.

Another awakening at 5:00 AM, this time to trudge through the woods stalking hunters. Make enough noise, we were instructed, and you'll scare away the deer. The hunters pointed their rifles at us and told us to get the hell on out of there. We kept following them.

We protested in front of fur stores in upscale shopping districts. We stood at the busiest entrance of the Pentagon shouting loud enough for the uniformed men and women to hear that the US Navy was using dolphins to find underwater mines and submarines. My mother never questioned the consequence of bringing her children to an anti-government protest. "We've got FBI files on us now," she told us, somewhat gleefully. "And your poor Dad always thought it would be because we're Muslims."

I started to crave normalcy, something that didn't involve getting out of bed before the crack of dawn and shouting at people in scary places. Those activities were important, but surely there were other ways to save animals. When the opportunity arose to volunteer for Lobby Day, which meant walking the halls of Capitol Hill and talking to Congressional staff about animal rights, I jumped at the chance. My father was proud of me. "It'll be a great experience," he said. My mother thought I was wasting my time. She believed in protests, direct confrontation. Those government people, she told me, were too corrupt to change anything. But as long as I was volunteering, she wanted her daughter looking sharp, so she took me to the mall and helped pick out my first black suit.

Decades passed with more protests, conferences, undercover videos, books, debates, insults, a few tears. My sisters both pursued careers advancing animal rights. My brother became vegetarian and his daughters raise money for beagles rescued from laboratories. Pakistanis, many of whom now have children involved in the movement, devour the soy chicken tikka my parents serve at their all-vegan dinner parties. My father's fears about the community were never fully realized – those Pakistanis who thought we were too radical were weeded out early. For the ones who remained, our crazy animal rights activities were overshadowed by juicier gossip over affairs, illegitimate children, and shady business deals.

Still, things can get awkward with the Pakistanis. It wasn't too long ago that one of the aunties showed up to my parents' dinner party in a full-length mink coat. I caught my mother in the darkened mud room where it hung. She stared at it.

"Mom, don't make an issue out of it," I told her. "You'll just make the guests uncomfortable."

"How can you be okay with this?" she asked me, reducing me to the cowardly daughter again. I explained that of course I wasn't okay with the fur coat, but there was a time and place for everything. When I went back to the kitchen, my mother grabbed the coat, took it outside, and shoved it in that auntie and uncle's car. Then she came back in and told everyone.

"But bajee," the auntie pleaded. "You know it's an old coat."

My father shook his head. I asked him later if he was mad at the auntie for being stupid enough to bring a fur coat to our house or at my mom for confronting her.

"Your mother is your mother," he said.

I understood what he meant.

When it comes to being a rebel, with my mother around, I never stood a chance. She was the rabble rouser. The renegade saving animals. Me? I played things safe. Went on to have a career as one of "those government people."

But it's funny when I think about it. My mother is Arnold, and I became a respectable member of society.

Maybe I rebelled against her after all.

The Fantasy of Normative Motherhood[1,2]

Roksana Badruddoja

My name is Roksana Badruddoja. I am a queer Bangladeshi-American woman, a mother to a precocious twelve-year-old girl who is negotiating her "brownness" at school, and a professor of sociology and women's and gender studies. And, I write today because I am worn out. I write with great pain and urgency fueled by restricting definitions of motherhood (and womanhood) which I did not create. Thirteen years ago, I made the decision to become pregnant; I made a choice. And, I did so without quite understanding the un-schooling that I needed regarding our cultural imaginations of motherhood (and womanhood). However, the onset of a high-risk pregnancy seven weeks into the first trimester changed my notions of what it means to be a woman, a pregnant woman, and a mother. This is the story of what I learned and un-learned, in the moments in which the fetus that resided inside of me was threatened, about what being a mother is.

I begin my story by arriving to my late twenties, when I found myself at the doorstep of the fantasy of normative motherhood. I inhabited an ideal-typical life as part of the South Asian American landscape. I was married – to a man, and he was employed, a Bangladeshi, and a Muslim. We purchased a home in an affluent Jersey suburb. We were healthy, we made our monthly mortgage payments and paid our annual taxes on time, we were over-educated with multiple graduate degrees, and we did not extend our "othered" religious and cultural practices outside of our private spaces. For a moment, I believed that I had completed my mission as the ideal Bangladeshi Muslim daughter and as an American offspring of the small pre-1965 immigration wave of "professionals" from South Asia. What else was there left to do?

It turned out, there was a lot left to do. I started realizing that in the society and family I lived in, not only was I explicitly expected to maintain patriarchy from within a heterosexual matrix, I was also implicitly required to conform to male privilege, white privilege, and capitalism. I was expected not only to have a baby, but to *want* to have a baby.

Here, as I draw on my memories of how I arrived at my decision to become pregnant, I have become acutely cognizant that perhaps my participation in the process of procreating had little to do with *my* biology but more to do with the biology of a social system informed by patriarchy, paternalism, and misogyny; white privilege and racism; and predatory corporate capitalism and class. In other words, because my body is sexed, gendered, raced, and classed in particular ways that fulfill the myth of the Model Minority, I am expected to become pregnant, carry my pregnancy to term, give birth, and raise the child from the birth. This is an essentialized definition of what it means to be an ideal-typical woman in America whose ultimate role is to be a vehicle for cultural (re-)production. I learned that my body was required to pass down traditions to subsequent generations (in order to shape ideas and feelings about race, ethnicity, and the nation).

As I was approaching my early thirties, I found myself "left behind" as I witnessed many of my female friends experience multiple successful pregnancies, purchase minivans with their partners, and fill their weekends with *Sesame Street Live!* I, too, began to imagine adding a child to our lives, and I set out in search of my "biological clock." While I was unable to uncover any "ticking," I felt (an invisible) pressure to catch up with my friends who had already had children. Hence, I announced to my then-partner that I was ready to become pregnant (even though I was fully aware that one of the implications of a pregnancy is giving birth to a human being for whom *I* would be fully responsible in a multitude of ways – something that still, at the time, made me somewhat uncomfortable). My partner was ecstatic; he wanted children. While I was pleased with his excitement and support, I also felt emotional discomfort. His response was simply, "I knew you would come around. *All* women, at some point in their lives, want to have children. *It's natural.*" The conflation between womanhood and motherhood coated with the stickiness of morality was clear to me.

More than a decade later, those words still haunt me. I am bitterly reminded of voices from my past: popular educational resources for expectant mothers, resources that imagined for me what I should want and feel as I became a mother. Motherhood seemed to be a glamorous and flattering addition to a woman's notion of self, á la Reese Witherspoon and Angelina Jolie. I imagined purchasing Juicy Couture diaper bags and Burberry onesies. I used Hollywood to glamorize the experiences of pregnancy (through predatory corporate capitalism). But, my pregnancy was far less opulent than this imagined truth.

My pregnancy was accompanied by physical and psychological debilitations that impacted my work, my relationship with my partner and immediate family, and my psychological and physical selves. By the end of my first trimester, I was ninety pounds (I had lost twenty pounds). The beginning of the second trimester revealed that the fetus was failing to thrive. I was in and out of hospitals for eight months (my daughter was born premature), and all the while, multiple intravenous lines and Reglan patches protruded from or were attached to my body. During my pregnancy, my body was unable to process any solids or liquids either for myself or for the life I was hosting within me. I became physically weak and dependent on others. I was unable to garner energy to lift my head. Walking a few steps to the bathroom became an immense task. My body was rejecting the pregnancy. For eight months, my daughter was nourished through hyperalimentation, an artificial supply of nutrients administered intravenously, while I was on bed rest. My partner left his job to stay at home with me, my sister flew in frequently from the Midwest to hold my hand while I slept, my father flew in from England every other weekend, and my mother-in-law left her partner behind an entire continent to care for me. Our worlds were paused so that I could deliver this baby safely without costing my own life.

Plainly, then, I was receiving conflicting messages: one from my body and mind, and the other from popular cultural imaginations. My lived experiences were uncomfortable and simply scary. A question that begs to be asked, then, is: what was I feeling during my pregnancy?

I wanted out! I wanted to rip my belly apart and expel the fetus from it. At times, I envisioned various methods of how to end the pregnancy, including throwing myself down the stairs. I became suicidal. My heart, body, and mind (and even my soul) were fragmented beyond reconciliation. That is, I felt that I – Roksana – no longer existed in time and space. In certain moments, it seemed to me that my daughter was directly looking at me with big eyes through the imaging screen, calling out at me, "Mama, it's me. Don't you recognize me?" I looked away every single time. She continued to persist, "MOMMY!!! It's me, it's me!" I did not want her to look at me. I did not want her to call out to me. I felt no positive emotions when I saw her legs trying to push through the taut skin on my oval-shaped, scarred belly, trying to kick. Rather, it reminded me of Sigourney Weaver's *Alien* (1979). I was terrified – not only of the medical complications, but of my own feelings. In opposition to how pregnancy was imagined for me by *What to Expect When You Are Expecting*, I felt empty and alone. I contemplated terminating my pregnancy.

Medical personnel at various hospitals I visited had little to no understanding of how a woman – a mother-to-be – could feel what I was feeling. My psychiatric evaluation report from one hospital with a nationally leading obstetrics department read "narcissistic and immature." Furthermore, my psychiatrist felt strongly that it was in my best interest to take antidepressants (Class C drugs that permeate the placenta); she was fearful that I might not be able carry out the remainder of the pregnancy without it. My OB/GYN, however, urged me to garner my inner strength and courage rather than consuming medications that could potentially harm my baby. Indeed, I became a reproductive threat and then an object of reform, a common cross-cultural imagination of women (of color).

Eight months later, it came time to deliver a premature but healthy baby girl. It was not until I touched my four-and-a-half-pound daughter – the warmth of her extraordinarily flushed, petite face against my sweaty cheeks; her tiny, salty and slimy fingers in my feverishly hot mouth – that I felt tender emotions for her.

It was *love*. What had happened? How could my feelings toward this child be so conflicted? I do not know what happened or whether I can ever reconcile my feelings. However, the experiences that were to come were even more difficult and confusing.

Hours after giving birth, I was unsure whether I wanted to nurse my daughter. I was uncomfortable with the idea. Perhaps I wanted to protect my own selfish desires and insecurities around my body. Perhaps the trauma of the pregnancy had left me afraid to open my body up to further abuse. When I thought about it, I realized that while all this time the child was medically in danger, this time, it was *me* who was creating a barrier to her being healthy.

What was wrong with me? What kind of *human being* was I? What kind of *mother* was I? What kind of *woman* was I? All these thoughts circled through my head and still, I couldn't bring myself to breastfeed. For forty-eight hours I "nursed" my daughter with a bottle.

It was only after I brought my tiny baby home that I attempted to give her my breasts. I chose to do so because I felt guilty for not even attempting to breastfeed her after she entered this world, and I felt that my then-partner judged me for making the decision to not breastfeed our daughter. However,

I was unsuccessful at nursing my daughter at home. I turned to pumping, all the while my guilt deepening. With a hospital-grade pump in hand, I produced less than two ounces of milk from each breast. I pumped for weeks and I simply was not producing enough colostrum to nourish my daughter. I felt defeated, as though I were being punished for initially refusing to nurse my daughter. I questioned my self-worth as a mother.

Eventually, my daughter and I worked out a feeding rhythm, and then a more comfortable mother-daughter relationship. But clearly, my experiences with pregnancy and its aftermath have had a profound impact on me, forcing me to re-think what it means to be human, a woman, and a mother. I am not sure that I will ever be able to come to terms with my pendulum-like feelings during and after the pregnancy. What I am left with, then, is an unanswered question: what does it mean to be a "good" mother (a construct horribly conflated with ideal-typical womanhood)?

I have come to realize that I've been asking the wrong question! The question of what it means to be a "good" mother assumes that the responsibility of mothering lays on one person in a male/female relationship: the woman. Karen Zivi (2005) points out that according to maternal ideology, "good" mothers engage in acts of self-sacrifice and self-abnegation, always putting the interests of their children before their own.[3] Moreover, this behavior of self-sacrifice and self-abnegation is presumed to emanate from natural instinct that at least all mothers should have, if not all women – an innate maternal instinct that should be guiding women to recognize their infant's well-being first. By implication, "bad" mothers are women who put their children in harm's way, either through a willful disregard for their maternal instinct or because they lack such instinct.

I have serious trepidations with the good/bad mother continuum because it does not reflect the realities of most women's lives, and it fails to recognize the vast range of mothering practices, particularly in the United States. Unmistakably, the assumption here is that mothers alone are responsible for their children, and it is through the portal of mothering that the regulation of women's bodies is justified.

In other words: I have come to realize that the immense guilt and pain I felt during my pregnancy and after my daughter's birth were feelings that had been put upon me by the society I lived in (and continue to live in), and also by the very specific set of "rules" that South Asian American families tend to abide by. My relationship with my then-partner and my family, not to mention my positionality in the world at large, led to much of my emotional distress at the time. I wish I'd had someone in that moment to tell me: this guilt is not for you to bear. This burden is not yours alone. You are not a "bad" mother. You are a mother, you are this child's mother. Nobody can take that away from you, and nobody can tell you that you are not doing your best.

I'm not implying that this realization has led to smooth and easy parenting. I have not slept soundly since I became pregnant over a decade ago. I continue to wake up sweating in the middle of the night because I feel ridiculously inadequate as a mother. I still rush into my almost-teenage daughter's bedroom apologizing to her silently as she sleeps, whispering, "I will never let anyone harm you, including myself." And as I look at her in the midst of the darkness, I feel shame. I am unable to look at myself lucidly in a mirror at times. I contemplate whether I should share with her the story about how our relationship began, how it might have almost ended. Will she hate me? Will she understand? Will she forgive me? Will *I* forgive my "narcissistic and immature" self?

These questions imply that there remains an absence of productive language that can be mapped on to motherwork that does not excise the messiness. I am hopelessly in love with my daughter and I would not choose a life where she is not present. I aspire to protect my daughter from harm and to provide her with a loving upbringing, and the life choices I make are often about what will benefit her. Yet, the notion that the category of "mother" is natural to the category of "woman," particularly in South Asian communities, is haunting to me. I cannot shake my nervousness when both men and women argue that motherhood (and nursing) are universal and natural phenomena for women.

My story is about being defeated, lost, and struggling while simultaneously celebrating, triumphing, and transforming. My hope is that in admitting to these dualities, in speaking out loud about the ways in which motherwork needs new language and more nuance, those women who feel as I have felt will now feel heard, and together, we will adapt our world to fit our needs.

Endnotes

1. Revised from "Contesting Maternal Ideology & the Yonic Myths of Motherhood: An Autoethnography," *Journal of the Association for Research on Mothering* (JARM), 10(1), Caregiving and Carework (Association for Research on Mothering 2008). Copyright © 2008 by Roksana Badruddoja. Reprinted by permission of the publisher.

2. This text was originally developed as a monologue for Yoni Ki Baat, sponsored by South Asian Sisters. The original piece, entitled "Contesting Maternal Ideology: The Yonic Myths of Motherhood", was performed by Maulie Dass at the Canvas Gallery in San Francisco, CA, on November 19, 2005. I would like to thank the women of South Asian Sisters Production and the amazingly talented performing artists of Yoni Ki Baat for providing me with a safe space to express myself.

3. Zivi, Karen. 2005 (November). "Contesting Motherhood in the Age of AIDS: Maternal Ideology in the Debate over Mandatory HIV Testing." *Feminist Review* 31, 2: 347-374.

The Photograph of My Parents

Neelanjana Banerjee

In the black-and-white photograph, my parents stand facing each other. You can make out the print on my mother's white chiffon sari and the dark frames of her cat-eye glasses. Her hair is in a bun. My father is a silhouette: a dark lean boy with one leg out, as though he was walking towards her. They are standing on a ridge of land. If you squint, you can make out stones, a smattering of grass on the dirt. A barren tree angles above them, cutting across the frame like lightning.

My parents had a love marriage. They met at Calcutta Medical College in 1963. My father remembers seeing my mother the day he had gone in for an interview. He asked her if she knew the questions they were going to ask. She said no. During school, they did not dissect the same cadaver. They may or may not have studied together. There were other women my father considered. My mother never looked at anyone else.

Once, when I visited India as a child, I sat with my father in a squeaky Ambassador on a personal tour of Calcutta. He pointed out a tree and said that my mother was standing beneath that tree when he knew he was in love with her. That memory flickers in my head as though it is playing on a filmstrip, at the end of a reel. The tree disappears in a flash of bright sunlight out of the window. Sometimes I pretend that the tree in the photograph is the tree my father spoke of that day, though I know it is not.

꽃

When I was twenty-three years old, I took the photograph from a hastily packed box in my father's study, where it had always hung on the wall in a cheap wooden frame. It lay like an accusation on top of miscellaneous file folders. I had come home to Dayton, Ohio, from San Francisco – where I had moved a year and a half ago – to clean out my room and help my mother move into a small, dark rental house five miles away. My father was going to stay in the house until it sold.

My parents were getting separated after thirty years of marriage. The divorce would go through later, but none of us could bring ourselves to use that word then.

I didn't ask anyone if I could have the photograph. My suitcases were bulging with elementary school memorabilia and old sweaters, the things that I thought would live in my parents' house forever. I managed to stick the photograph in anyway.

Back in San Francisco, I rolled the overstuffed suitcase into the back of my closet, and tried to shut the door. I worked long hours at a weekly Asian American newspaper. It was 2002. There were a lot of stories to cover: The Patriot Act, INS Special Registration for South Asian and Arab immigrants, the escalating wars, Flying While Brown. After work, there were underground parties in the Tenderloin or at warehouses in Oakland. I learned to drink whiskey, neat. I kept *The Ethical Slut* on my bedside table, used it as a manual to relationships.

My mother called me from that lonely house, her voice shattered. Mostly, I kept the situation with my parents at a distance, but at the end of a long night, I felt like a tight rope walker who suddenly looked down to find that the net had been cut away. Suddenly, everything was off balance.

Late at night, I would pull the suitcase out and look at the picture. It made me angry – an image constructed of lies. I imagined spitting on it, shattering the glass – my hands bloody. But then I would just pack it away again.

꽃

Growing up, I chafed at my parents' suburban immigrant lifestyle. They were both physicians, and I went to a private college-prep school. There was a lot of: "You have to be ten times better than your 'American' classmates." We don't believe in "learning from your mistakes" they said. "We can't afford to make mistakes." I raged at the tennis-playing Indian kids, who were all going to become doctors. I yearned to move to New York City. I read Jack Kerouac obsessively, smoked shoplifted cigarettes, or – in high school – dirty brown weed out of a makeshift tin foil pipe, leaning out of my bedroom window. I didn't want anything to do with who my parents were.

In college, I sought out drugs and other distractions, and began exploring non-monogamy. It was easy to lie to my parents and, therefore, to others. I was practiced at it. My boyfriend, a white boy from Portland, Maine, who taught me about jazz music and film and how to carefully break someone's heart, pushed me to grow up. He told me that until I stopped lying to my parents about everything, I would never be whole. He and I broke up in the spring of my junior year. I was cheating on him with a golden-skinned lacrosse player. In the heart-rending conversations we had that spring, the boyfriend said some harsh truths. I decided to go home and really talk to my parents, really talk honestly to them about who I was, who I wanted to be, and the way I saw the world.

It never happened. For the first time in my life, my parents seemed preoccupied with themselves. My father kept insisting that he was going to die soon, that he was tired of the private practice he had built over the last twenty-five years as a beloved internist, that he wanted buy a boat and sail around the world. My mother, a pathologist, had been in the Air Force for many years and only recently switched to a private lab associated with the hospital where my father also worked. She was at the high point of her career. She had no interest in giving it all up. At first, my father's laments seemed funny. Then, somehow, they became triggers for arguments my parents couldn't seem to move on from. I'd seen them fight before, but not like this. There was no room to bring up the conversations I had wanted to have about myself.

My mother's mother was sick that summer, dying. She left to visit her in India, and I decided to take my father out to lunch and talk to him. My father had gone on a service trip to India when I was a child to volunteer at a leper colony. My plan was to remind him of all the good things he wanted to do in the world. I remember feeling so sure of myself walking into that Chinese buffet. "Just go and volunteer again, Baba," I told him over a plate of crab legs. "Stop all this nonsense." He looked me straight in the eyes and told me that if he went, he felt he wouldn't be able to trust himself. He followed up with: *Do you know what I mean?* I remember how the slimy, corn starchy buffet slop congealed in my mouth. Three years later, my parents were divorced.

After the divorce was official, my mother still called me crying. She had endured the last few years of personal anguish; now she had to deal with the public shame of it all. The mother of one of my best childhood friends from the Bengali community was visibly shocked when I told her that my parents' marriage was over. "Chi chi chi," she kept saying over and over, tears streaming from her eyes. I think she meant that it was a shame that such a strong relationship could fall apart, but my mother took it as a personal attack. She stopped going to any social functions. She couldn't escape at work either. My father had abruptly retired and moved away. She began avoiding the doctor's lounge, took the stairs instead of the elevator, kept her head down. When some doctor, always a man, would corner her, loudly ask her where her husband was, my mother developed a deadpan response. "I don't have a husband," she would say.

My father had left her for a nurse that worked in his office for many years. Someone I had grown up with, who would come to our house for our annual staff cook-out, and who knew exactly how to draw the blood from my grandmother's weak veins. She was working-class, blonde, with a scratchy smoker's voice. Once, over too much sickly sweet Pink Zinfandel – her wine of choice – she told me how getting into a relationship with my father was the best thing that had ever happened to her, how thrilled her family was. I wanted to be angry, but I just felt sad.

❧

For years, that moment in the Chinese buffet with my father haunted me. How blue the sky had looked before walking into that restaurant. I remember how nonchalant I was, as though I understood the world. And then, it went spinning off its axis. I was twenty years old, always precocious, and right then, I wanted nothing more than to go backwards, to become a little girl again, to cover my ears and scream.

It is easy to rebel against your Indian parents, for an ingrained generation gap and their irrational fears and strictness. In fact, it seemed like it was what I had built much of my sense of identity around. But what about when your father looks you in the face over crab legs and admits to being human? My mother was worse. I empathized more with my father, and that was the worst thing I could have done. And suddenly, I didn't want to fight with her anymore. How can you be disobedient to a mother who confesses that her heart has been completely broken?

❧

A year after the divorce, I started working at a youth media organization where I helped young people tell their own stories: boys who had been shot and lived with shrapnel inside their narrow chests, girls whose boyfriends pimped them out on MySpace, children who were kept in cages in youth prisons – people with real trauma in their lives. I lived in the middle room in a first floor flat in an old Victorian near Dolores Park, with a window that faced walls. The photograph of my parents hung next to my bed, above a vintage lamp my ex-boyfriend from college had given me. I wrapped the lampshade in a red duppata to soften the light, but I kept the top open and it shone a spotlight there. I was forming new one-on-one relationships with my parents; adult relationships, ones predicated on all the ways we had failed each other. We weren't equals, but we were trying to be friends. When I looked at the photograph then, I no longer only saw my own shadow reflected in the glass. I could see that it was a photo of two very different, very young people full of flaws and dreams and future betrayals, but also so much hope. The photograph felt precious then, delicate as a newly laid egg – or the very pink skin under a peeled-away scab.

My mother only lived in that dark rental for a year and a half. She moved into a sunny yellow house with an open floor plan, which she paid off fully in five years. She spends her time with a diverse community of friends that she met through yoga. They go kayaking on the Little Miami River, and chant on New Years. She is lonely, but fiercely independent.

My father and his girlfriend live in Sarasota, Florida – in a house with three cats and a dog. They grow fruit trees on a piece of land out in the country and sold their boat a few years ago. I guess he didn't want to travel the world after all.

When I met my husband Robin, I had an overwhelming urge to tell him all that I had learned from watching my family fall to pieces, and then reconstitute. He listened, and still does. It took me a long time to feel ready to get married, but sometimes, I think it was the photograph that convinced me.

I keep the photo of them in what used to be my office, before my son was born. Now, Robin and I sleep in there, and Kai has taken over our bedroom. I often think about how many tiny moments have to happen to produce a human being. The photograph seems illuminated, bursting with possibility. I hung it on the wall next to my writing desk. It serves as a reminder to take risks, and no matter what may happen, not to be afraid to love.

The Politics of Being Political

Piyali Bhattacharya

It starts with a drone strike. Or perhaps it starts with the hashtag #BlackLivesMatter. Sometimes, it just starts with a word – race, class, caste, gender. But no matter how it starts, I always know how it's going to end: with an email from my mother.

> Piyali,
>
> I saw your latest Facebook post, and I'm writing to tell you that it wasn't appropriate. You don't have to listen to me, but really, why must you waste your time with all this political commentary? Are you a politician? Are you a reporter on CNN? It doesn't suit you to be constantly ranting on Facebook and Twitter about the inequalities of the world. Yes, we all know that sexism and racism exist. But why must *you* always be the one to make such a noise about it? Have you ever stopped to imagine what your male friends or your white friends must think of you? Every time they see you post an article they must think, "Well, this is yet another reason not to be friends with a nag like Piyali." Have you forgotten that you grew up in white society? Have you forgotten that some of your closest friends are white, and that your father and I came to this country and survived and prospered because of the welcoming soil of the U.S. and the support and friendship of, amongst others, many, many white, male colleagues? How do

you think it feels for us to see you relentlessly posting articles that often belittle the people we hold dear – people who wish nothing but the best for you?

If you won't stop posting these ridiculous articles for your own sake, at least consider your parents. And besides, how can all of this posting be good for your career? Do you hold a degree in political research? No, so it isn't as if your thoughts are the results of serious examination. It isn't safe for you to be opining on all these things about which you're so ill informed on such a public platform. You're a fiction writer! Do you want people thinking, "Oh, there's that girl who is always more interested in showing off her opinions than actually writing a heartfelt story?" If you want my opinion, enough is enough.

Achchha, don't forget to respond to the other email I sent you about Rasika Aunty's daughter's wedding. Can't decide what to wear, have sent you pictures of two different saris that are possibilities. And take your vitamins – because of vitamin C, I didn't get a single cold last year. I'm telling you, it really works, listen to your mother! And call me when you get this.

Love,

Ma

❧

People say that the natural progression of life is that you rebel against your parents when you're a teenager. Then, after college, you start realizing that you rely on your parents more than you thought you did. By the time you're in your thirties, it finally dawns on you that your parents only had your own good in mind all along, and you come to rely on their sage advice as you navigate your way through adulthood and maybe even a parenthood of your own.

I'm not going to say that my progression through my teens and twenties was opposite to this trajectory, but in certain ways, it veered from this path. I knew when I was very young that I wanted to be a writer. When other children played catch outside, I hid in our home library with books. I wrote my first short story when I was seven. My parents were unendingly encouraging of my interests, taking me to bookstores on weekends and creating long reading lists of novels they thought I'd enjoy. My mother, who herself had several literature degrees and had pursued writing professionally until she'd had children, was thrilled that I was following in her footsteps.

When I went to college, I found myself in a difficult position with most of my Desi American friends. They spent a large part of their lives lying to their parents. We had deep heart-to-hearts about how they longed to tell their parents that they didn't actually want to be doctors or lawyers or software engineers – how to tell them that they really wanted to be painters or social workers or teachers. But I always felt on the outside of these conversations because my parents had never stopped me from pursuing an English major, or from studying literature abroad at Delhi University. Conversely, they often asked me how many sources I was using for my latest paper, what my creative writing workshop had said about my latest story.

But their reaction to my work was about to change. I moved to New Delhi after college to pursue a career in journalism. At school, I'd imbibed philosophies I had never before been exposed to: I'd discovered feminism, I'd learned that the personal was political, and I'd believed that my opinion could make a real difference. These were all the empowering messages that I would pour into hard-hitting articles when I made it as a journalist. Armed with this naïve conviction, I packed a bag and headed across the planet. My mother may have said everything she wanted to about Delhi being an unsafe city for a single, American woman whose Hindi was only somewhat fluent ("Why can't you at least move to Calcutta, where we have family and where you speak the language?"), but I was ready to take the Indian capital city on.

This in itself was disturbing to my mother, who couldn't understand where my interest in "writing" had turned into an interest in "journalism."

"Journalism is for people who keep up with the news," she told me. "Fiction is for storytellers."

I shrugged her off and moved to Delhi anyway. Once there, I started making friends with academics, journalists, and policy planners. My conversations with them opened me up to worlds I hadn't known existed. My phone calls home started to take on a new tenor:

"Ma, have you been following what's been going on with the Delhi state elections?" I would ask.

"Since when did you start taking an interest in politics?" she'd respond, before quickly switching the subject.

It would take me years to understand why she was so eager for this "phase" of my life, as she read it, to be over, when she had never before had a problem with any of my choices. For years, I was puzzled by her attitude as she continued to be very proud of my accomplishments, but to engage only mildly in the work that I found to be vital. I spent a long time being frustrated by our conversations, wishing we had more common ground in this area. Only recently did I realize that I, too, was partially responsible for her reactions to my choices.

"You were such a sweet child," I grew up hearing. Quiet, respectful, with native fluency in Bengali, appropriate skill in music and dance, and good grades, I was exactly the daughter I was raised to be. I had never so much as asked to hang out at the mall after school. I had never given any indication of being anything other than the perfect Good Girl.

I now realize that when, at eighteen, I morphed into an opinion-wielding feminist, I surprised my parents. They were taken aback at my sudden firm-footed hold on the world, my determination to live a big life that spanned the whole planet, not just a happy life that took me, at most, one hour's driving distance away from them.

I understand their shock, and even their hesitance, to watch me go down that road. I may not have been alive the day that my parents packed their suitcases, said tearful goodbyes to their families, and got on a plane to fly eight thousand miles away to a land in which they knew nobody, but that moment in my family's history will live inside of me forever. If I should ever have children, that moment will live inside of them, too. The debris that scattered in that rupture has nestled into all of us; it guides all of our decisions.

But my reaction to it is the opposite of Ma's. The day she left her country was the day she signed the contract affirming that she wouldn't be there when her mother died or when her father fell ill. She can think of no better future for me than to do exactly the reverse of what she did: to hunker down and live a small, quiet life somewhere close to where I grew up.

I, on the other hand, yearn to catch all the sunlight and all the pain of the world in my hands. To this day, I believe that involving myself in the ecosystems around me and immersing myself in the most raw parts of life is the only path to human healing. That is a cause I find to be worthy enough to kick down the doors of my comfort zone and let distress and heartache in.

So, that's what I did. But it was not something my parents understood. One of the first pieces I ever had published in a national Indian news magazine was an opinion article on how I felt about India's involvement in Kashmir after I visited the Valley – namely, that the Indian Army had unnecessarily turned the Kashmir Valley into a terrifying police state and that, before anything else could happen in Kashmir, the Indian Army needed to remove its troops. My parents called me after the op-ed came out, distraught.

"Is this how we raised you?" they asked me. "We raised you to take sides against the country we come from? We raised you to go around publishing rubbish about things you don't understand?"

We argued for days. They were angry that I had exposed my political feelings to the public, and sad that my opinions were so contradictory to theirs. Worse, they felt that I would one day regret my open, "radical" behavior. It was one of the first times I realized that though I had made it through college thinking that my parents were not the types to draw lines in the sand about what I was and was not supposed to do, the truth was that their lines just weren't in the same places as other parents' lines were.

Our conversations about that particular article ended with them telling me that while they were proud of me for having achieved a major publication, they still didn't know how to feel about what I had written. It was to be the first of many times when they would be torn about my success.

❧

By the time I moved back home to New York, I had trained myself to keep tabs on several newspapers a day, and I relished my newfound ability to plug into conversations about almost anything that was happening around the world. I had developed opinions on the politics in both countries I belonged to, and I became involved in campaigns, protests, and petitions. I wrote freelance articles for a number of liberal and feminist publications. I left my fiction in my bottom drawer and savored my new role as an essayist and commentator.

Through all of this, my mother asked me to keep in mind where my real talent lay.

"You are a storyteller," she reminded me. "Do you really fancy yourself writing these one-off essays for the rest of your life? Where is your book of short stories? Where is your novel?"

She wasn't wrong. By this time, I was in my mid-twenties and had, perhaps unsurprisingly, married a political scientist. After holding several jobs in journalism, I'd taken a job in Editorial at the press affiliated to the University where my husband was a professor. The job was what I was educated to do, but publishing manuscripts daily only reminded me of how badly I'd once wanted to publish one of my own.

At the encouragement of my family, I decided to quit my job and apply to MFA programs in creative writing, to see if I could get some time and some guidance to write the novel I'd been thinking about for a while. When I got into a very prestigious and competitive program, my parents were thrilled. "What is the book going to be about?" they asked. "Can we read it?"

Yes, I needed to tell them about it and they needed to read it – mostly because I really needed their help. My book was to revolve around what were, in my opinion, problems with American immigration policies. It was going to follow characters both from the Model Minority population of South Asian America and from lower income households, some of them undocumented. I was particularly interested in what happened with these characters at the time of their retirement – what did it mean for immigrants who had spent their whole working lives in the US to retire, and how did that picture look different for "model" immigrants than for those who were undocumented? Additionally, I was interested in how immigrants of all stripes interacted with the American healthcare system – an issue very much stimulated for me by conversations I'd started having with my father, a doctor. This story would require so much research, and there were no better interviewees than the two people who I had seen experience many of these hardships first hand.

Still, I found myself hesitating for a moment before delving into explanations of my work. This was not going to be the "lovely story" that my mother so wanted me to write. How would my parents feel about my taking on such a project?

I shouldn't have been worried – they were incredibly supportive. Maybe they had started to expect that I might write something like this, but I found them bubbling over with ideas to share with me, even giving me people to contact when I went on a long research trip that took me first through all five boroughs of New York City and then to Nepal, Bangladesh, and India.

As I delved further into the world of undocumentation and healthcare, as I traveled and read and researched, I thought about how these issues were interconnected with so many others. No social concern exists in a vacuum – after all, there's a reason why such a large percentage of people who don't have access to healthcare in the United States are people of color, or why the lack of documentation for a subsection of our society often leads to a whole host of other problems that affect *our* daily lives as American citizens. As I started becoming more and more involved with the people who were living and thinking through these dilemmas, I felt myself becoming more vocal about what I witnessed in the world around me.

But "vocal" is not a word one associates with a Good Girl.

As my personal worldview was expanding, so were online spaces like Facebook and Twitter. Through these forms of social media, I found myself having access to communities I might previously not have been able to reach. All of a sudden, if I had a question about my research, I could access this network to find someone who might answer me and maybe even be willing to meet with me and introduce me to others that I could then interview.

I started following online the papers and magazines that dealt with the topics I was researching and I met more and more people who were interested in similar things. Soon, I had a morning ritual of scanning my news feeds for interesting articles and links that friends were posting, reading them and reposting them myself, to make sure that word was getting out about all the social issues that so many of us were spending time researching and writing about.

This reading and sharing of as much knowledge as I can gain access to is still a part of my daily routine, and it is maybe the thing that bothers my mother most about how I approach my career. To my mind, all of the articles I read, all of the discussion threads I post to or post about, they all enhance and are a part of my daily work. I could not write what I do (in non-fiction *or* in fiction) if I weren't regularly involved in these conversations.

Moreover, my discussing or posting thoughts about people from a certain demographic in no way prevents me from being friends with that demographic. My writing about men and women and my posting about white people or people of color in this country in no way precludes me from feeling a great deal of love for my male or white friends.

None of these things, however, make sense to my mother. To her, fiction is fiction and politics are politics.

It's ironic to me sometimes that I could never have been the person I am today had it not been for my parents' overwhelming support. I think back to those childhood evenings spent in bookstores and libraries, to those summers they had me spend in India so that, in their words, I "developed a real relationship to the country, not just a relationship to India forged through songs and movies." I think back to their relentless pursuit of the best education for me, of their deep desire for me to be happy in what I do.

It's ironic to me because without that kind of encouragement, I may never have had the guts to discover all these sides of myself. I may have done what I think is the secret desire of many Model Minority mothers for their daughters – gotten married, had babies, and pursued a part-time career on the side of throwing elaborate birthday parties. I may have had the *easy* life that so many immigrants dream about for their children. And I understand where that dream comes from. I so deeply sympathize with the longing of an entire generation of immigrants to see their children taking advantage of their sacrifices, to see the next generation not have to face the hardships that they did. That whole generation, after all, left their homelands "for the sake of their children."

So I understand that part of my mother's hesitation with regard to what I do is that she finds it so *difficult*. To choose a tough career (which will not simply be a secondary career to my husband's), and then to choose to have a political opinion – I see that part of her pain in this comes from the fact that she sees me struggling and exposing myself to judgment, to hurt. And it kills her. I see that.

But, funnily enough, she is the one who enabled me to be an independent woman, and a woman who was not afraid of confronting the world and myself in it. Unsurprisingly, that attitude has seeped into everything I do, into everything I write, whether it is a novel or a Facebook post. And some days, it breaks my heart that Ma still considers my politics to be so outside of my work and myself.

Recently, I've considered not sharing my views with her, maybe even blocking her from seeing certain things I post on social media. But every time I come close to hitting the "hide" button, I find myself unable to do it; mostly because she doesn't deserve that. Both my parents have been so unfailingly supportive of my career, even if they cannot understand my specific opinions within my work. When I told them that I was publishing a book called *Good Girls Marry Doctors* which would revolve entirely around South Asian American women and their parents, my father told me: "Write your truth, and it will be beautiful." My mother cried the day I showed her the book contract for this volume. "You're an author," she said, smiling.

But more importantly, I can't imagine a life in which my parents and I simply won't talk about the things that are important to us. Certainly, family dinners would be more peaceful if we could all manage to keep our mouths shut about our beliefs. If we wanted to, I can see us slipping into safe, frothy conversations while stealthily building walls around our hearts, making sure our emotions don't seep out. But that is not the family my parents built, and it's not the kind of relationship any of us want.

So maybe I have a few more uncomfortable emails regarding the impropriety of my views coming my way. But maybe that's not such a bad thing – as long as we promise to always keep those lines of communication open.

Fair Game

Madiha Bhatti

Once upon a time, at the appropriate and understandable age of thirteen, I was a *Twilight* fan. Whenever I leafed through its pages, the image of the vampire heartthrob's first cautious steps into sunlight stood out to me. I remember reading those sections and sympathizing with his hesitation, "He must be worried about getting tan." In the fictional world of *Twilight*, the most beautiful characters aren't just white, they're *alabaster*, and it's the perfect shade of pale. In the real world of a first-generation Desi, the same standard applies. The centuries-old conventions of beauty imposed by colonialism are as undead as Edward Cullen and his coven. In my life they've been kept alive by the expert (disproportionately doctor) hands of resident uncle-jis and aunty-jis.

Nearly thirty years ago my parents left their families and friends in Pakistan and crossed the pond to the land of the melanin-free and tanning-bed brave. They are your standard immigrant prodigies, they toiled, creating successful lives from scratch while managing to raise well-cultured and unentitled (I'd like to think) children. But they are not your neighborhood uncle and aunty. My mother is a dynamic matriarch who seamlessly balances cultures. She is a woman who tried to dissuade me from studying medicine, manages to have non-skittish conversations about sex, concedes that the race of her prospective son-in-law shouldn't be a deciding factor, and allowed me to live and work abroad for almost two years. As far as the standard pressures imposed by Desi parents, I've won the lottery. Most of my youthful rebellion skipped straight past them and landed in my local Pakistani "community."

In an ideal world, referring to the adults in your life as "uncle" and "aunty" should create a sense of affection and community that transcends generations. In actuality it is a social contract, in which the beta or beti will be subjected to a lifetime of unsolicited scrutiny, a favor they must repay by inviting said aunty or uncle to their wedding, where aunty-ji will criticize the venue, overly familiar banter between the happy couple, and the bride's makeup. Aunties in particular have a middle school bully's eye for physical flaws. In my ugly prime, I had a frizzy bowl cut, an eczema rash, glasses, and a semi-permanent scowl from my life-shattering seventh grade angst. I am aware of this phase in my life primarily because of the photo evidence and secondarily because aunties were constantly trying to rescue me from puberty with verbal disapproval.

Aunty critique comes in four flavors: direct, indirect, retroactive, and comparative. These are examples I've received of each;

Direct – "Beta don't crinkle your nose when you laugh, it will give you wrinkles."

Indirect – "Is your hair naturally that thin?"

Retroactive – "Oh thank goodness, your skin has finally cleared!"

Comparative – "Her face looks so fresh, you would look like that if you spent less time in the sun."

In the mind of an aunty, these comments are productive; they see themselves as lifelong personal trainers who are motivating you to get into rishta (proposal) shape. As you fumble through an adolescence of diets, hair straightening, and eyebrow grooming, they are at the other end, waiting to take credit for your transformation.

I give them some measure of credit for my childhood fear of the sun. I can't pinpoint the moment in my life when I looked in the mirror and decided I was *too* dark. It was just an understood truth that whiteness was synonymous with beauty in my community. Mostly, I have scattered memories. Affection and attention being heaped on children with brown hair and fair skin. Friends refusing to join the pool party for fear of getting dark, or being visibly whiter week after week as whitening creams surged in popularity. Every time a new daughter was married into a family I heard the same hollow conversation:

"How is she?"

"Beautiful. Very fair."

We outwardly joked about the absurdity of it, but for years I couldn't spend a day in the sun without coming home and scrubbing until my skin was raw.

In the modern American context, the desire to be white seems somewhat out of place. Most of us have experienced some form of admiration or envy of our wonderfully ethnic, chocolate, caramel, chai skin by our marshmallow, cream puff, low fat milk peers. (The weird fetishization of brown skin is another rant entirely.) Yet those voices were drowned out by the expectations of a community that took all the liberties of an extended family and gave none of the love. A generation of impressionable girls were handed down their mothers' insecurities, and we good South Asian daughters took them without complaint.

My actual extended family wasn't without influence. My paternal grandmother was as light as light gets, with blue eyes to boot (I hesitate to admit this: I think Desis secretly love to brag about that blue-eyed member of their family. It's like an admission that says, "This is in my gene pool, play your cards right with me and there's a .0000001% chance our children will look like Kate Hudson."). I have cousins who aren't just pale, they're *alabaster*, and I've watched them grow up with excess attention, and go through life taking extra precaution to keep it. I have cousins who are dark, and were aware from a young age that that was not a good thing to be. And I have cousins whose mothers coat them in mercury-laden skin lightening creams day after day because, as much as they loathe white-washed culture, they don't mind white-washed skin.

The measures these families take to keep their daughters fair range from ridiculous to dangerous. Through my years of experience as a South Asian daughter, I've collected the advice of aunties to better navigate the road to a fairer and lovelier complexion. At first, I started creating these lists out of a sense of survival. But when the weight of them started to overwhelm me, I tried to look at them with some humor.

Things that will make you look lighter:
- Stand next to a very dark person
- SPF 200
- Only take photos with a blindingly bright flash
- Use foundation/makeup that matches the whites of your eyes
- Agoraphobia
- Apply "Fair and Lovely" on your face until it matches no other part of your body
- Play a version of "don't step on a crack" where you only walk in the shade
- Stay under an umbrella

Things that will make you look darker:
- Direct sunlight
- Indirect sunlight
- Standing next to a very white person
- Shaving your legs
- Swimming
- Every other conceivable outdoor sport and activity

I had no weapon left other than to make these lists funny – it made the grim reality more palatable. I'm not saying there aren't still days when I wear more sunblock than is medically necessary. Being comfortable in all the shades of my skin is a work in progress. But I recognize what is at stake: South Asian daughters are being taught to hate their skin. Their self-worth is being tied up to pigment, and it's a slow-working mental poison born of blatant critique and favoritism. Our rebellion needs to be two-fold: against the community voices that create a narrow and impossible standard, and against the voices in our heads that keep us from loving our skin in all of its natural winter-pale and summer-tanned glory.

An uncle once explained to me the difference between shukkar and chini, brown and white sugar. "Brown sugar is natural sugar, it's raw and healthy, but not as nice to look at. In white sugar, they add chemicals to bleach it, but it's sweeter in its natural form." The irony was not lost on me. Wherever we fall on the color spectrum, we South Asian daughters have a responsibility to love ourselves in shukkar form and to demand the same love from our communities. Heartthrobs or not, we can no longer derive our standards from vampires; it's time to kill the monsters of our childhood, once and for all.

Daughter of Mine

Meghna Chandra

In the summer of 2012, over the space of an afternoon, I nearly became a mother.

I was going to start my senior year of college in a few days and was visiting my neighbor Kim before I left home. Kim handed me a beer and we got to talking. She asked me how I was, and I casually mentioned that I was having irregular periods and that I was going to get an ultrasound that evening to check for irregularities in my uterus. Kim looked at me strangely and asked in her Boston accent, "Well Meg-i-na, are ya sho you're not pregnant?"

"No. Noooo, definitely not." I had never even considered it as a possibility. It seemed completely ridiculous. I slung at her reasons why it couldn't be true: I got my period after having sex. I hadn't felt any symptoms. He didn't come inside. And wouldn't I know by now?

"Well, I never felt Sammy at all that time, even though Sean was playin' basketball in there. And some women are weird, they get their period all throughout, or maybe what you thought was a period was just spotting. Have ya had any weight gain?"

Yes. Yes, I was having weight gain. But I had figured it was because I had just been in India being force-fed enough for a baby elephant.

The possibilities started to turn over in my mind, and I could feel my eyes bulging. "What about an abortion? I can get an abortion, right?" I thought of it as a last resort, like paying $25 for a new college ID.

"Well, sweetie, if it was four months, then you are havin' that baby!" She

45

pulled me into the kitchen and she handed me a pregnancy test. "You have to know." She said to me squarely.

I drank six cups of water from a magenta Beauty and the Beast cup. Squatted over the toilet three, four times with my legs spread, stick positioned to catch a flood of life-deciding fluids. I felt a sharp twinge of pressure, but no fateful fluids were forthcoming.

I stumbled out of the bathroom and wandered back to the porch. I told Kim that my ultrasound was coming up in half an hour, and she said, "Don't bother with the urine test then, the ultrasound will tell you for sure."

I walked back home from my neighbor's house, shaking. My mother greeted me at the door, ready in her Costco track pants and supermarket floral shirt. "Are you ready?"

"Mom, I can go myself. I don't want you to worry about it."

She harrumphed, "No Meghna, I am going with you, you don't have a choice. Ashada madri behave panna kudadhu." Don't behave like a moron.

I couldn't think of anything to say, so we went to the car together, as we had done a million times before. We pulled out of the garage, and I swallowed dry gulps. I calmed down and started to deliberate. *Maybe I'm not pregnant. Maybe I'm completely overreacting.* In the car next to my mom, I mentally combed through my menstrual history.

I don't think I've had my period since the first week of May. I thought back. *Maybe I had it in June. Don't I remember thinking that I was NOT pregnant in Calcutta and celebrating quietly with some spiced momos? Maybe, maybe not. Not in July. Not in August. I last had sex on May 10th, which may or may not have been with a condom after I stopped taking birth control... I just don't remember.*

What I did remember is my aunt straining to button my new sari blouse over my breasts, which were suddenly spilling over C into D territory. I remembered feeling nauseous the day before.

A sudden pressure in my stomach became a little foot kicking at my uterus.

We pulled into the parking lot, and I did my best to keep my breathing shallow and my pace even. The atrium and corridors of the hospital blurred. I sat in the waiting room next to my mom, who was writing Sri Rama Jayam in her notebook again and again. I felt an impulse to join her in a frenzied return to the Gods I had intellectually disavowed.

I furtively reached under my shirt and explored my abdominal flesh. It seemed thicker than I remembered. The flesh felt more muscular. A fleshy fortress for baby?

I recalled the ancient trope of the mother falling in love with her baby as soon as someone puts it in her arms. I imagined myself as a teen mom from one of those MTV shows who everyone cheered on for their courage, but who no one wanted to be.

I hate you, I hissed internally, pressing down on my abdomen. *LEAVE.*

The water I drank earlier pressed down and I went to the bathroom as Amma continued to write Sri Rama Jayam. I looked at the mirror and became determined to face my radically changed reality.

OK, so if I am pregnant, how will I have this child? I tried to think of some kind of precedent for my pregnancy, which, at this point, I was almost completely sure was underway. The only other scandalous people I knew at the time were a few girls from high school whom I had never talked to.

But no Indian girls. In my mind, Indian girls never had unprotected sex outside of marriage. They never deviated from their paths towards engineerdom or doctordom (it was bad enough that I was determined to be a labor organizer). They never fucked up royally, as I clearly had.

Having lived in India for two years, I now recognize the absurdity of being afraid of what "Indian girls" do or do not do. Brownness does not mean homogeneity; brownness is not fixed in some idea of chastity. There is probably no such thing as brownness. But at the time, I thought that I needed to find someone like me, who had a mother like mine.

The only example I could think of was Kunti from the Mahabharata. Kunti, the mother of the Pandavas, had her first son out of wedlock with Surya, lord of the Sun. Panicked, facing lifelong disgrace (who would believe he was divinely conceived?), she gave birth and abandoned her child by a river. The royal charioteer found the baby, a beautiful boy with skin the color of Amul butter on toast, and adopted him. Karna went on to be a great but tragic hero.

I will be Kunti, I decided wildly. *I will go to Philadelphia, drop out of school for a semester, and live on Julia's farm in Oklahoma. I'm over eighteen; the school doesn't have to tell my parents anything. I will deliver a tea-colored baby and drop it on the doorstep of some yuppie couple and get on with my life.*

I went back to the waiting room with new resolution. A receptionist called my name ("Meg-a...MAG-na?") and my mother and I followed her.

The ultrasound technician greeted us and smiled so pleasantly, I felt bad that I could not smile back. My mother made to come into the room with me, and I burst out suddenly that I was too embarrassed for her to come.

She looked at me worriedly. "Kanna, don't be scared! I will hold your hand!"

"No Amma, really, I'm embarrassed, I'm sorry."

The ultrasound technician broke in and explained to Amma that technically, legally in fact, she wasn't allowed to be there if I didn't want her to. Amma frowned and I could tell what she wanted to say, but in the hospital the letter of the law trumped maternal law.

She scuffed her shoe on the floor and said, "That's why I came here; I thought you wanted me to be with you."

"No Amma, no really, I'll be embarrassed, please, *please*." And since she actually had to listen to me, she shrugged, sat back down, and resumed writing Sri Rama Jayam in the waiting room.

Me, who walks around the house naked, embarrassed?

I entered the ultrasound room on my own and felt the weight of the door between me and my mother. Once in the room, I did everything the technician told me to do. Gown tied, feet stirrupped, bottom down, relax, relax, breathe.

"So I'm here because I have irregular periods. After I got off birth control. It's not weird, right, lots of people do?"

"Hmm? Yes sweetie, now I'm going to put this tube in, but I'll do it slowly and I'll tell you when I'm doing everything, okay?" *So amicable, this one*, I thought. Push, angle, OW, I stared at her face for gasps, or knotted eyebrows.

"Umm, do you see anything I should be worried about?" She explained as she already had that she was not allowed to tell me anything legally because only the radiologist is supposed to interpret the images.

Saved by the first legal technicality, damned to limbo by the second.

More angling. *Ow, is sex so painful? I forgot; it's been so long. Well, I am never having sex again if this thing blows up.* She sucked the probe out.

"Thanks for warning me about everything." I told her. My voice was still very high.

She snapped her gloves off. "No problem, sweetie."

"Um. Umm. Did you... did you see anything that could look like a fetus?"

She stopped for a second, astonished. She beamed. "I *thought* you were nervous! No, sweetie, nothing at all. Why, are you worried?"

In place of my water breaking, my detailed sexual history rushed out from between my stirrupped legs. She assured me, "Don't worry, if there had been anything there, you would have seen it for sure."

We both went out, she smiled at me, but I didn't smile back because I was terrified Amma would pick up on our shared joke and ask me about it. Amma lifted up her bag like it was a sack of rice and asked me how it was.

"Fine, but they won't tell me anything until Monday." She didn't answer and drew her lips tighter together.

Ah, so it seems there is a price to pay. I tried to explain why I wouldn't want her in the room with me, but she kept looking ahead. Maybe she was thinking about how children branch off from their parents and remain forked from each other forever. In this country where daughters deny their mothers entry to their transcripts, bank accounts, medical records, and ultrasound viewings, what did being a mother mean anyways?

I asked her why she was so quiet. "Poi tole." she said. Get lost.

I got angry. She was always emotionally blackmailing me, making me feel guilty for exercising my legal rights to privacy, having sex, staying out late, going to protests, having adventures in far-flung places. "We have sacrificed so much for you children, and you are so bloody ungrrrrateful." She spat again and again whenever we fought. Was the price of being an immigrant's daughter perpetual obedience and lack of control over my life? What if I wasn't willing to pay that price?

Now, I have realized that neither my mother nor I can hold ourselves hostage to some ideal of a sacrificing, pious, grateful, obedient, chaste Indian girl, an idea that many people in India do not subscribe to, and which has rarely, if ever, described actual women's lives. Things have changed since we left India in 1993; mothers are different, and daughters are too.

Even so, I'm not sure that I understand my mother and why she looked so hurt when I pushed her out of the ultrasound room. She is fond of saying, "You will only understand when you are a mother."

I found out weeks later that my irregular periods and weight gain were symptoms of Polycystic Ovarian Disorder. This means I may never be able to conceive a child. The curse I put on the baby in the waiting room of the digital imaging office may have actually worked.

I put my hand on my stomach and lift the curse from my imagined child. *I do want you so someday I can be your mother and love you and stay as close to you as I can, even though you'll branch off beautifully and courageously towards an autonomous life in which you are free to do stupid things and have pregnancy scares and make the world your own. You are mine, after all.*

Flipping the Script
Finding the Love of My Life While Writing the Book of My Heart

Sona Charaipotra

If you ask my father, he'll tell you that whatever he asked me to do, I did the opposite. And I guess, in a way, that it's true. He wanted me to be a doctor – a pediatrician, specifically – so I could take over the practice he and my mom started in Central New Jersey some 30 years ago. Instead, I buried my nose in books, threatening to become an English major. When he insisted there was no career in that, I instead turned to journalism – since it had a job in the title. Then, instead of working at *India Abroad* (run by my uncle, the CFO) and making my name "in the community," I interned at *People* magazine, and eventually worked there, writing fluff about celebrities my father wouldn't be able to begin to name. When he said go back to school to get a masters, I did. To study screenwriting. And then again, to study fiction. You can see where this is going.

But perhaps our biggest point of contention was in another realm of my life altogether. From the time I turned twenty, my dad (and my grandmother before him) fretted about my marriage prospects. I had so much stacked against me: I'm only five feet tall. I have too many useless degrees. I write about celebrities and TV for a living. Who would ever want me?

So my dad made it his mission to find me a husband. And I rejected his options at every turn. We've all heard the stories: surprise guests showing up for dinner, unknown numbers popping up on your cell phone. Emails from eligible strangers. It was relentless. And I foiled him every time: skipping out before the dinner guest could arrive, deleting messages without reading them. There were long silences. There were shouting matches. By the time I was twenty-eight, he was good and stressed.

Little did he know, I'd long been channeling my singleton angst into my grad school thesis project, a very autobiographical script about Anamika, a twenty-nine-year-old single Desi journalist in New York whose dad gives her the biggest deadline of her life – find herself a husband by the time she's thirty. Or he'll find one for her. I called it *-30-,* after both the old school journalism "end-of-story" marker and that dreaded, looming age, the one at which a perfectly smart, beautiful and funny protagonist (or, you know, human) gets dubbed an old maid if she's not rocking a ring.

There was Hollywood interest in the script, though in the end it didn't make it to the big screen. (A story for another day.) But oddly enough, on that very trip to Los Angeles: a plot twist.

I met a boy. He was smart, he was funny, he was charming. He was a chatterbox, although nerves made him quiet on our first date. And he ate dessert first. That was it. I was smitten. At twenty-seven, I had met the love of my life. And he was Indian! By twenty-nine, I was married – in Vegas, just the two of us, although of course we didn't tell anybody that then. And months later at twenty-nine, we had the proper big, fat Indian wedding, planned, delightedly, by my parents. Which is not to say there weren't still a few snags in Daddy's eyes. For one, Navdeep is two years younger than me. (I know: sacrilege!) And he, too, is a writer. If my dad knew what headdesk meant, he'd be doing it right now. At least he's brown though, and not Gujarati. My mom wouldn't know what to do with herself if she had to "make sweet food," a common stereotype about Gujaratis and their cuisine.

So what did that mean for my fictional Anamika and her grand dilemma? When I started the script, at twenty-four, I thought I was writing my life story, thinly veiled. But by proverbial and literal thirty, I had actually done one thing right, in my father's eyes, at least: I was married. How could I write this story when my own life had flipped the script, so to speak? The anxiety I once felt right down to my very bones had drifted, dissipated. I was no longer that girl.

So I turned to other works, flitting from project to project, learning that we all have many stories to tell. And I even found another story that could maybe become "the book of my heart."

But all that while, Anamika and her angst remained stashed in the back of my head, sneaking out every so often to remind me of its existence. And recently, I realized that, while my own tale had taken a turn, Anamika's story is still very relevant, maybe now more than ever. Because she still exists. She's a part of me, the girl I was, the girl who made me who I am today. And I see her in my sister, who now bears the brunt of my dad's stress about her prospects, even though she's uber-successful and smart and beautiful – and dare I say, fulfilled. I also see Anamika in countless brown girls across the country who are feeling stifled by parental pressure.

I see her in non-brown girls, too, who feel the weight of that ticking clock, of societal norms and expectations, of the idea that they'll never be complete without a man and a ring and babies to go along with that six-figure paycheck and spotless McMansion.

Unraveling all this in Anamika's story, I've learned the hard way that, when it comes to fathers and daughters, it's never going to be easy. I may have found the husband, but we're a pair of writers, which means I've dashed Daddy's dreams of tucking away with the grandkids in the in-law suite in that still-MIA McMansion. He's proud when he sees my book on shelves, but he'll never stop worrying about where my choices will take me – and, perhaps more importantly, where they will not. I'll never quite live up to his expectations, and like that twenty-three-year-old version of myself, I'm learning again to embrace that fact – as long as I can live up to my own.

That's why I've recommitted to sharing Anamika's story – still, in so many ways, very much my own. Distance has perhaps made her narrative clearer, sharper, the sting not so strong, the pinch not so harsh. I can see the humor now. And, really, I can see my dad's perspective now, too. How, like most fathers, he was just doing what he thought was best. How, now, as a parent, maybe I would fret over my daughter's (and son's) future too, hoping that they'd find a partner to share their journey with. Don't get me wrong – I still see the errors he made, in thinking I wasn't good enough without a man, that my own successes couldn't remedy that flaw. But I hope, maybe one day, when he finally gets to hold that book called -30- in his hands, he'll finally be able to understand my perspective, too.

Good Girls Become Doctors

Sayantani DasGupta

On a warm summer afternoon when I am seven or eight, I am alone in my room playing Barbies – those sexist, bad-for-girls'-self-image dolls that my activist mother hates. Through my open windows, I hear a woman screaming.

"Stop! Stop!"

I rush to my window. A man and woman are struggling in a car across our quiet suburban street. I'm not sure what is happening, but know that there is something wrong. She is crying so much; shrieking, really. I run down the stairs.

"He is killing her!" I announce, glassy-eyed and short of breath. I am more than a little proud to be delivering such obviously important news.

My mother leaps up, yanks open the front door, and makes to dash outside, toe-ringed bare feet and all. A family friend – a fellow Indian immigrant and a professor at the university where my mother is a graduate student – is visiting. He grabs hold of her arm, and urges my mother to stay inside, to stay safe.

"Why get involved in these Americans' problems?" he asks, or something to that effect. "Let's wait for the police."

However philosophically sound, detachment is not in my feminist mother's vocabulary. She brushes off such concerns and, after commanding me not to follow her, runs across the street. It turns out the couple, grown-ups to my young eyes, is actually a pair of teenagers. In an era long before dating violence was on our common cultural radars, this is what I have witnessed: a young woman getting beat up by her abusive boyfriend in his parked car.

Within a few days, I am put in a karate class offered by the university where my mother is finishing her psychology PhD. I am not a naturally athletic child and would far prefer to do something more sedentary and stereotypically "girly" – reading, playing with my dolls, making grotesque-colored potholders on my loom-maker. But I am not given a choice. There is no doubt, the incident has shaken something loose in my parents, something they do not name, but that hovers around the house, both angry and worried. I do not fully comprehend it, but I know it all has something to do with me. I realize the world is a more complicated place than my hitherto humdrum existence of lemonade stalls and Brownie troops has led me to believe.

My mother continues her feminist activism, while I continue school, karate, and dolls. Her feminist consciousness-raising group meets occasionally in our house, and sometimes she takes me to a Take Back the Night or similar rally. Activism becomes such an integral part of our household culture that I hardly notice it. Ideas about gender equality are mixed into my morning cereal; principles of social justice are woven into bedtime lullabies.

A few years later, I am taken to a sexual assault seminar. In the second wave feminism of that era, such events were usually all-woman affairs. But my mother has insisted that my father and Bhaskar, the same Indian professor friend, come along as well.

"It is important you know what we women face," says Ma.

The men are made to stand in the back of the room, so as not to disrupt the all-women's space. There were also, in retrospect I assume, no other people of color there except my family contingent. Are you surprised? It was, after all, the 1970's, in the heart of the American Midwest. Feminist spaces were not particularly diverse at that time.

To this day, I can remember being terrified by what I heard. At twelve or thirteen, sex was barely on my radar, beyond the mechanics of intercourse for baby making. The notion of giving in if my assailant had a weapon was terrifying. Being taught to feel a rapist's body for identifying moles or scars was almost too much to bear. But I learned more easily digestible self-defense information as well: how to park under streetlights or near open shopping stores, to hold my keys between my fingers such that I can use them as a weapon, to never stop by the side of the road for a police car if I was alone, but to drive slowly to the nearest police station.

At the same time, feminist consciousness was not something that was solely Western-flavored. I was taught throughout my childhood about my revolutionary grandmothers and great-aunts who fought for India's independence. I am particularly taken by the stories of Banalata DasGupta, my paternal grandfather's sister, who was imprisoned by the British for revolutionary activities and died in her early twenties of something as curable as goiter due to lack of medical care in jail.

When I travel to India over my long summer vacations, I am regaled with such tales and with images of maternal strength. These stories are writ both large and small. From the ferocious power of the warrior goddess Durga, whose image decorates every Bengali home and is an omnipresent part of my cultural upbringing, I am equally taken by my grandmother's stories of learning to ride a bicycle during the revolution. She tells me how radical it was at the time for a woman to be independently mobile, to travel around without a male relative's escort. I learn to connect such acts of personal empowerment to the broader swath of local and global politics. Bicycle riding is as important as taking back the night, I learn. Autonomy and agency is a first requirement for any meaningful feminist or other social justice action.

Eventually, my mother grows disenchanted with the mainstream feminist movement's lack of racial and other intersectional politics. When my family relocates to the East Cost of the U.S. for my father's job, she forms "Manavi," the first anti-violence women's group in the South Asian American community. The organization is literally a homegrown affair. My father draws the Manavi logo and helps my mother with publicity and other administrative issues. We hold meetings in our house. I stuff envelopes and sell samosas at the group's first fundraiser.

My mother's activism is both accepted and not entirely palatable to our immigrant Bengali community. By bringing something as taboo as domestic violence to the light of day, Manavi risks undermining our community's carefully cultivated 'model minority' face. But my mother walks the tightrope between her feminist activism and her immigrant identity with aplomb. She is both a mild-expressioned, sari-wearing, daal-cooking wife and mother, and a radical whose razor tongue takes no prisoners. My father, for his part, takes any community ribbing about his wife's activism with a joke, cold shoulder, or sardonic smile.

"We should form a men's group, called Manav, eh?" they ask, poking him with an elbow.

"Why?" Baba asks, "Isn't patriarchal society enough of a men's group already?"

People eventually stop asking stupid questions. My father is not the kind of person that people mess with anyway.

Fast-forward a decade. I am a college student, and my father is trying to persuade me not to go into English, but medicine. I am outraged. I fall easily into the narrative of oppressed immigrant daughter, and try to frame my father's advice as backward, immigrant claptrap.

"This is my life," I howl. "These are my dreams."

You know, standard, selfish brattiness. I am so misunderstood and all that.

But it's the politics that eventually wear me down. I know, as does my father, that his advice doesn't come from any backward-thinking place, any desire to keep me under his thumb or control my "dreams." They come from an understanding of gender inequality, and the importance of women's economic autonomy to their lifelong agency.

"I don't want you to ever be dependent on a man – or anyone – for your livelihood," my father says, "I want you to always be able to stand on your own two feet."

As immigrants, my parents had nothing to give me but my education – there was no trust fund, there were no network of colleagues to help me make college or job connections.

Economic independence is at the heart of a lot of immigrant dreams – kids becoming doctors, lawyers, and engineers. But at least for me, becoming a doctor was also not just an immigrant choice, but a feminist one.

Subterfuge
On How to Be Obedient
While Rebelling

Tara Dorabji

The art of subterfuge is passed through generations of women on both sides of my family. Sometimes, we use it to avoid judgment, other times to get what we want. My daughters learn this quiet art. We rebel and we are obedient. Subterfuge is part of my core, no matter how hard I try to slice it out.

Grandmother, the flavor of rebellion that brands me must've come from you. You died before I was born and took your secrets with you. Did you really have an affair that ended your marriage? I have your letters that you wrote to my dad. I have your saris that my mother saved. I wear the cream silk one with the maroon and gold brocade. But I don't have answers or memories, just pieces of you, jagged reflections that are a part of me.

I find you in broken stories written in blue ink on translucent paper. All the key players are dead. You are so lovely in your photos, like an Indian Jackie Kennedy, short skirts and thin legs, a handbag and scarf to match. No matter what, you kept up appearances. This is the mark that separates our generations – the careful attention to how others perceive us, the need for bragging rights, the determination to put your best foot forward at all costs, no matter what you were doing. It is the first law of subterfuge: look good, so you can do what you want and avoid the judgment.

You divorced your husband. This was unheard of in India at the time. You lost custody of your children and moved to Mysore where you met an Austrian man with yellow teeth and dreams of chasing gold. He loved you.

He married you. You were the first to marry outside the Parsi community, but you "married up," or you married light. You married white. So this was okay, even if it severed ties to our community. To be Parsi, your father must be Parsi, but you already had your children. So, maybe marrying outside didn't sever the bind to our cultural line. Somehow, you committed the ultimate rebellion and came through smiling in those photos. You looked so damn good.

Your son followed in your footsteps. He married my mom, a European girl that he met at the I-House at UC Berkeley. I could still be Parsi, technically. But I was raised Catholic. I was raised white. I search your letters as if they could uncover those whitewashed pieces of me. You were thrilled that my parents married and wrote to my mother:

> I am very happy that my son has a good girl, cultured and highly intellectual! The best thing that I like about you is that you are fond of cooking and take great care of my son. He praises your cooking very much!

I read this over and over. How happy you are about my mother's class and that she will take care of your son and cook for him. Her education seems a necessary decoration. And for a while it was. My mother played the executive's wife. She perfected each dish to my father's discerning palate, adding a bit more garlic, less toasted cumin, grating in fresh coconut. My father wore tailored suits, silk ties, and glasses with thick rims. My mother donned saris at parties. The Indian men in Western suits, the white woman sheathed in silk fabric, exposing a swath of cream skin.

My parents kept up appearances at all costs. They never fought. The danger of subterfuge is that you forget you are lying and start believing. Every night my father would come home from work at 5:30 PM and kiss my mother on the cheek as she finished cooking dinner. It is all that I remember of my childhood – onion sizzling in oil.

One morning, my parents sat us down on the black, leather couch. The grandfather clock ticked on the wall. I pulled an orange and gray afghan blanket onto my lap, covering my bare legs. I was still in my pajamas.

We are getting divorced. The façade of order shattered in four words. My father demonstrated this separation by bringing his hands together at the palm and then driving his fingers in opposite directions. *We are two people that went our separate ways.* No one in my school had divorced parents. It was something I only knew about from after-school specials. I went into my room, got into bed, and pulled the blankets over my head. I would never talk about it. I would go on as if nothing changed. I was seven. I would ask no questions. Still, a darkness sank deep into my stomach, getting heavier and heavier. I closed my eyes tight, willing me away. What bothered me most was that the future went on interminably. I would never escape this.

My mom worked double time after my parents divorced. On Tuesday and Thursday mornings, I got ready for school all by myself. I had my own key and locked the door when I left. We moved across the street from my school and my mom remodeled the house while we were in it. I remember us sleeping outside in the backyard one night because every room was torn up. I never questioned any of it. There was a simple rule: follow my mother and move forward despite exhaustion. We pulled wallpaper off walls and painted the house inside and out. It must have been a cleansing for my mom. And afterwards, she was reborn. She dated younger men and had single, women friends that talked about everything. Juicy details that my twelve-year-old ears absorbed greedily – middle-aged women finding their boyfriends cheating, or leaving their abusive husbands, or getting fired from their jobs. Always the conversation revolved around food, my mom's cooking still the center of family life. Sometimes, I put my hands over my ears and said, *Mom, stop!* when she discussed her sex life. I mean, some things you just don't want to hear. Still, in those stories shared around the table with a piping hot pot of tea, my mom expressed her ultimate dissatisfaction with love and men. It was the first sign that she was not perfect, a crack in the façade. The first dent in the silent canon of rules.

My dad remarried and plunged deeper into the river of American assimilation. He wore blue shorts and Velcro; he stopped wearing a tie. The quiet, calm, emotionally austere experience that marked my life as a child got shaken up when he married a twenty-seven-year-old woman from Vegas with two kids. The house screamed. Kids punched holes in paintings. Dirt tracked through the house. From his new wife, I learned about cake mixes, microwave dinners, and pop tarts. We went to Disneyworld, Great America, and the San Diego Zoo. I ate it up and relished my stepmom's tales of kissing boys at twelve.

Even with the influx of new experiences, the expectations from both my parents were uniform. Get good grades and stay out of trouble, at least trouble that could be seen. My mother and I operated on *Don't ask; Don't tell.* The first law of subterfuge was still in order. I kept it looking good.

I maintained the most important surface layers – good grades and not getting caught. But I was part of the grunge generation, so that impeccable surface layer gave way to faded flannel shirts with holes, baggy jeans, and, eventually, body hair. I rebelled, but was just obedient enough. Rebellion and obedience are two sides of the same coin. And this was the currency for cohesion in our family.

I started small, lying to avoid consequences. I lied about bike rides, claiming to go to a friend's house. Adrenaline coursed through my veins as I sped two miles down Bubb Road through the suburbs to the 7-11 to buy tons of candy and keep it under my pillow. By high school, I had carved a pouch in the chair in my room to keep my pipe and weed hidden. Older boys, late nights, cars, and railroad tracks. I refined my rules of subterfuge. You must believe that what you are doing is right for you and that someone else knowing will only hurt them. The lie is love. It works best when everyone believes it.

Did you run your life like this, too, Grandma? Were you having an affair? Was there an undercurrent that I will never know? Did my grandfather know? Did he leave it alone as long as you came back to him? What happened to push it over the edge so that you would divorce in the India of the 1950s? What made it worth cracking the veneer of perfection and respectability? Was it a dream that drove you or a nightmare?

During adolescence the gap between who I was and who my parents believed me to be grew. So much needed to be hidden. Boyfriends were allowed, but weed was not. Would I pull a Bill Clinton and claim that I didn't inhale just to keep the peace? Christmas Day of my freshman year in college we got caught taking bong hits in the bathroom at my dad's house. Well, technically, I didn't get caught. My two sisters did. The eldest sister took the heat and swore she was acting alone, but I was getting older and didn't feel compelled to lie. I told my dad that I smoked pot. I never told my mom. She wasn't there. Why did she need to know? It went against everything she believed to be true. Maybe I only confronted subterfuge when I knew I could slide by.

In college, my life aligned. I followed my passion and dug into the movement. We staged sit-ins and teach-ins. I was on the front line in Seattle when the World Trade Organization was shut down. I believed so much in who I was and what I was doing that I didn't want to hide those rebellious bits of me. Or maybe those were the parts of me that I could get away with exposing, the acceptable rebellion. The other parts I still hid – the partying, the one-night stands – the pieces that were too difficult to justify, but still existed.

In some ways, I loosened the grip of the first law of subterfuge – I didn't need to look good on the outside because I felt so damn good on the inside. But there was, still, a deeper law to subterfuge that had me in a noose. The second law of subterfuge is tricky. It's about manipulation – the way you act to get what you want. As daughters, we are trained to be gentle, to be soft, to put others' needs ahead of our own. Don't be abrasive to achieve your goals. Parts of me were still deeply obedient to the family, to my role as daughter. I paid close attention to the subtle expectations of when to call, of how to receive advice, of when to serve, and how to give. These controlled my inner compass. In effect, I was trained to please, to meet the needs of the family. *No* was not a part of my vocabulary. I was dutifully trying to balance everyone's needs.

It's not something that all women fall prey to. I wonder about you, Grandma. Could you balance your needs or did the family come first? I have painted this picture of you as a renegade chasing your own dreams. I wonder if that made you happy. Or did the pain of losing custody of your children overshadow everything? I imagine you to be well trained at female tactics in communication. Complimenting men, suggesting things conditionally, manipulating to get your way.

Our rebellion builds over generations. It's funny to think how for you, divorce was an ultimate rebellion, but for my generation no one bats an eye at divorce. I didn't get divorced, but only because I didn't get married. I had kids out of wedlock. When I separated from my children's father there was a seed of rebellion and a finding of my voice. I see a pattern across our generations, how in our separation or divorce from the men who fathered our children – we find our voice. At least my mother and I did. Did you, too, Grandmother?

Can you imagine how much has changed in just two generations? I had kids without being married and hardly experienced a sideways jab. I separated from my kids' father when my daughters were four. I was eight when my parents divorced. I think my dad was six when you left.

My kids' dad is brown. Would this have bothered you? His family survived the war in El Salvador. His mother is illiterate. Together we crossed all lines. Our children can navigate across boundaries and borders.

But we ended. Parts of me were dying inside. These were quiet days and years that led up to the sudden announcement that we were separated. It wasn't subterfuge; it was survival. We yelled and screamed. Gave each other the stink eye for days. But some decisions you have to make on your own. I had to find my truth. I had asked so much of my family in accepting him and welcoming him. Over the years they had grown together. I dropped the news of our separation like a guillotine. I didn't deliberate or seek council. One day we were over, and I rode it out long enough to make sure it would stick before making the announcement.

My mom got right behind me and put her support there. The conversation was short. She offered one piece of council, relaying a conversation she had with my ex, just saying that she wanted me to know what he had said in case it offered me new perspective. I explained my decision in a few sentences, and she said, *Then it's over and I am behind you.*

Your son wanted to advise me, to weigh the options together and make sure this was the right choice. *Sometimes, I think I could have worked things out with your mom,* he said. I think he believes you could have worked things out with his dad. In that moment, I was disobedient and blunt. I broke the second rule of subterfuge. I chose honesty. I was not soft or sweet. I told my father, *I am not asking for advice. I made a decision and this is a notification.* The subject was closed. I rebelled more in how I told my father my decision than in seeking the separation. I was not gentle.

I am done with subterfuge, or at least I am trying to be. Or maybe I am just lying to myself and pretending to be, holding tight to the silent canon that is still deep within me, relinquishing bits of what is hidden when I know I can get away with it.

And who will I become when my daughters are teenagers? In what ways will their rebellion flatten me? Things did not go so well with my son. He rebelled his way right out of my household. Calls from school and police, pipes, weed, knives, and cutting. Nothing is more devastating than realizing that you cannot save your child from himself. Losing the closeness that we shared when he was young is one of my greatest pains. I wonder how I could have reached him. In the end there was nothing left but to let him experience his own consequences. To let the rebellion go full throttle.

Some days, I cling to my absolutism. I want to be perfect so my children will have something to duplicate. I know this is wrong. I know I must fail and that they will learn from this. It is survival.

This is the ultimate break between my generation and yours. When I sit down with my friends, I don't try to shine the light on my life that shows them the best pieces of me. I go to the sorrow. I go to my weakness. I go to the pain. Because this is where I am most real. This is where I want to cast light. This is what binds us together.

In the end, I want to be real and perfectly flawed.

Good Girls Pray to God

Triveni Gandhi

When I was sixteen, I decided to stop eating meat. Well, rather, stop eating chicken since cows, pigs, and most other animals were already off the table. At that time, my mother was the only vegetarian in the house as my dad, older sister, and I all indulged in sinful butter chicken and more. My decision to stop eating meat came out of nowhere really – there was no spiritual awakening nor ethical considerations. I just hadn't eaten meat in a few days and did not really missed it at all – so I stopped. You could say I quit cold chicken.

My decision was widely lauded by my mother, grandparents, and various aunts and uncles. Though my family descends from Punjab (the eat, drink, and be merry capital of the world), most of them follow a strict Hindu lifestyle. Choosing not to eat chicken anymore was seen as a way of abiding by traditional Hindu principles and, by extension, obeying implicit family directives about appropriate religious beliefs and practices. While I had always been somewhat religious growing up, the added validation of my new choices further solidified my stance as a more devout Hindu. Ultimately, having my elders whom I love and respect take a sense of pride in my decision made religion and family obedience intersect in a way that impacted me for many years to come.

One of the earliest stories from Hindu doctrine I remember is about Ganesh (the elephant God-king) and his younger brother, Karthik. Both children were considered wise in their own ways, but the sage Narada (known to be mischievous) decided to test the young gods to determine who was wiser of the two. Enticing the boys into competition, the sage offered a boon of knowledge to the first boy to circle the earth three times. Karthik immediately raced off to complete the rounds, but Ganesh chose to go around his parents three times. He reasoned that as his parents, they were his world, and in doing so won the competition.

Though a seemingly innocuous story, fables like this had a profound impact on me growing up. Not only were my parents and elders supposed to be my entire world, but they were also the closest I would get to God on Earth. I came to see disrespecting, disobeying, and lying to them as nearly a sin – because it was a direct assault on God. It was as if my relationship with religion was mediated by the relationship with my family – if an elder was upset with me, it was as if God himself was upset with me. Similarly, my religious practices and choices (such as meat eating) were a part of my identity as a "good" daughter. Choosing not to pray at the temple in the evening, or not knowing the words to certain prayers, carried emotional guilt, while being able to demonstrate devoutness or religious knowledge seemed to add brownie points to my status as a respectable Indian girl.

Moreover, the idea of India and what made me "Indian" was entirely dictated to me by my family and their belief structures. While I visited the country at least once every two years growing up, my experience with the broader idea of India was always moderated by religion and cultural expectations. I remember long lazy summers in my grandmother's home, indulging in sweet mangoes and spicy pickle in the cool blast of the AC. With my parents as chaperones, we would visit family members, go shopping, and see movies. Many trips included religious pilgrimages to different Hindu landmarks across Northwest India. While they seemed exotic and new, in retrospect these experiences always fell within a certain cultural and religious boundary, handed down from my grandparents to my parents to me. In many ways, I saw India only through the one lens of my family, specifically the Hindu Punjabi upper-class lens that left little room for other lived experiences. Certainly I knew that there were other religions, cultures, and castes in the country. Yet knowing those things existed did nothing to change my perception that following the beliefs and expectations of my family is what made me "Indian."

It's clear to me now that this relationship between two such large forces in my life necessarily conditioned how I thought about myself. Dogmatic ideals found their way into my everyday behavior, and in some ways I used them as a way to stand apart from others. I remember frequently asking fast

fast food workers to change their gloves, clean their knives and boards, etc., when I ordered vegetarian meals from them. I ate up pseudo-scientific stories about how humans are not meant to eat meat from my religious uncles, and I silently nodded along when other family members claimed that people who ate red meat were inherently violent because of the extra hot blood coursing through their veins. Being vegetarian, Hindu, devout, and an all-around good girl gave me a sense of identity and satisfaction that I was special and above others. Ultimately, this sort of dogma allowed me to justify my social exclusion from the other "cool" Indian kids as a measure of worth as I struggled with insecurity and self-doubt. Whenever I felt confused about where I fit in American and even Indian-American culture, I knew that I could fall back on those comforting cultural and religious rules handed down to me.

These feelings of religious-derived superiority continued until I turned twenty-one. At that point, I was scheduled to finish a joint BA/MA from college, had already applied to PhD programs around the country, and had lived at home my entire four years of undergraduate education. My familial obedience and devotion to God were unquestioned. Yet, there was a sense of something missing, a feeling that no matter how good I was, things tended to fall apart. In the months leading up to my birthday, as my grandmother passed away, my mother lost her job, and I was betrayed by a loved one, I felt as though things were spiraling out of control. Despite all that I had tried to give to some higher power, the worst seemed to find its way into my otherwise unmarred life. In retrospect, perhaps these trying experiences could have been an opportunity to renew my faith in the God I was raised to believe in. In reality, as a young woman approaching a huge milestone in the American way of life, they made me feel as though I needed to reconsider what I knew so far. I felt tired of constantly trying to maintain a position of superiority over others; I was weary of trying to live up to an ideal of what "perfect Indian daughter" meant. Most of all, I was exhausted from the emotional rollercoaster I was on. With all of this plaguing me, I decided that when I turned twenty-one I would start drinking alcohol.

Now, alcohol plays a similar role to that of meat in my family. Not necessarily disallowed, but definitely not sanctioned. It was also a point of pride to not be a drinker, and there were some who looked down their noses at others who drank inside and outside the family. When I studied for four months in France, I chose to drink wine with my host parents, chalking it up to a cultural experience. After that, however, I didn't think much of it. Religious members of my family didn't approve of it, hence God wouldn't either. Like eating meat, it was a vice, a temptation and a poison, the avoidance of which only made me a better person. But as I approached my birthday, something about the turmoil around me and the fear of my life post-graduation made me feel like I was not that superior person I always thought I was. If bad things happened to me, that meant I was just as morally corrupt as the rest, and so why not indulge? On my birthday, I went out with my close friends, my older sister, and her husband, and, under the guidance of these elders, I drank. It wasn't especially remarkable but it marked a change in the way that I thought of myself and what God meant to me.

This change and confrontation continued when I started graduate school eight months later. Now I was 1,700 miles away from my place of birth, my family, and the small pond I had been a big fish in. Navigating the new waters was challenging in many ways, and not having a community I could rely on around me made it difficult to stay connected to the person I always thought I had been. Add to the fact that I was no longer in the protective bubble of other Hindus – my new social group was predominately white and atheist, or agnostic at the least. This is not to say they were and are not tolerant of different viewpoints, but that they challenged parts of religious culture that I had previously taken for granted.

For example, many Punjabis believe that Mondays and Tuesdays should be considered "holy" days on which neither meat nor alcohol should be consumed. This meant when I joined my classmates for a drink after our late night class on Tuesdays, I'd order a ginger beer. My friends questioned why religious principle only applied two out of seven days of the week, or on the full moon once a month, or during religious festivals that came a few times during the year. If I drank alcohol or ate eggs otherwise, then what was the point of abstinence during certain mandated days? How was God okay with indulgence in certain sins on some days and not others? These were questions I had perhaps thought through my years but had not explicitly confronted in the confines of a fairly strict household. As I entered a new sphere that challenged my assumptions and self-confidence, I could feel my faith quiver, and sometimes slip away.

Short trips to India over the summer were no help. In graduate school in America I was becoming more liberal and opening my mind to new ways of thought, but in India I felt an inextricable need to conform to the ideas I had been raised with. I had to prove to my family and to myself that being born and raised in America did not make me any less Indian, any less Hindu, or any less obedient. Even as I matured, my understanding of India and Indian values was conditioned on how people around me allowed me to experience these things. As I grew closer to a "marriageable age," I remember people commenting on how "Indian" my sister and I were but not knowing what that really meant beyond being obedient and superficially religious.

Being in India helped me feel reconnected to the person that I always thought I was, the younger me who knew exactly who she was. Yet this reconnection created more contradictions for me. If I could be one person in America, and another in India, then who was I really? Where did my faith actually lie, and what did my different actions and beliefs in varying contexts really say about who I was?

In some ways it felt as though there were two Trivenis – one who was "herself" when she was on her own, and the obedient, religious, good Triveni when she was around family. These two women were irreconcilable in my head, and so my faith in God became the battlefield for a much larger personal struggle for self-definition. In some ways I felt it would be easier to return to the principles of the past with rules that I already knew, yet I also knew the rigidity of those beliefs stifled me and made me feel more distant from my spirituality. I went through cycles of trying to adhere to old principles, then forgoing them for what felt right at the time, followed by huge burdens of guilt, shame, and self-loathing for not sticking to my guns like a good Indian girl would.

Interestingly enough, it was during ten months of fieldwork in India that I was able to come to terms with what religion, family, and spirituality meant to me. I lived in Jaipur, Rajasthan, a good deal away from most of the relatives that I usually visited on trips to India. Though I lived in a women's hostel, I had an aunt and her family who lived nearby who I would see often. My bua (or father's sister) and her husband are deeply religious, but in a way that felt much more personal than I had experienced in my immediate family before. While they did impart religion-based rules on their sons, similar to my upbringing, I never sensed that religion and obedience were tied together. Both my cousins were spiritual in their own ways, and it wasn't forced upon them. When I participated in religious ceremonies or went to temples with them, I didn't feel compelled to see God the same way they did, and for the first time in a long time, I really thought about what this entity means to me, not to me and the rest of my family.

The ten months of traveling from village to village, managing researchers, and having vast experiences with Indians outside of my family structure transformed my vision of India as a whole. For the first time, I had the emotional and physical freedom to try new things, see new kinds of places and interact with a wide range of people on my own terms. While some elements of India definitely carried over from the way my family had filtered the country to me, I was able to create a new relationship between the Indian experience and myself. It was around this time that I started a romantic relationship with my partner, a boy raised in Delhi but who had cultural roots in Kolkata. Learning about a new, non-Punjabi culture was critical in helping me reach a broader understanding of what India is and what it can be. Between the Rajasthani culture I was learning about every day, my Bengali boyfriend, and a new sense of emotional freedom, my perception of India became just that – mine. While I'm not entirely sure anyone can understand the mystery of India, I do finally feel that whatever I know of it is my own, seen through my own Indo-American eyes.

More importantly, during this academic and emotional transformation I was truly able to sort out what God meant to my sense of self. I came to understand that my religious practice did not have to be expressed in a certain set of outward behaviors, but rather I could have a personal, spiritual relationship with this higher being. Moreover, this sense of spirituality had to be directed inwards to attain any true strength from it. All my life, I had felt that God cared about the way I behaved towards and with other people, with no regards to how I treated myself. It was when I was at my lowest point during the strenuous toil of dissertation research that I realized I first had to be kind to myself *and the God within me* before trying to please anyone else. Before seeking the goodness and Godliness to respect in others, I had to find the God within me and cherish that. Finding that sense of self was crucial in my self-definition, and I finally felt free from burdens of expectations and truly accountable for my actions and beliefs.

Today, I observe certain religious practices, like not drinking on Mondays and Tuesdays, not out of guilt or religious belief, but out of respect for my family's beliefs. Though I may not agree with everything they do, I know that I love and respect the God within each of them. At the same time, I also know when I have to acknowledge my needs first, such as my decision to re-incorporate fish into my diet for health reasons. Even though I still do not eat meat, I've made that choice an ecological one rather than moral or religious. But when I am home visiting my family, I will go with them to the temple and participate in religious ceremonies because I know it is important to them and I love them.

Looking forward, I wonder whether my ability to navigate the various forms of religiosity will stay with me. I see my parents and other elders around me become more religious as they grow older, and Hindu traditions that are linked to certain family principles are much more solidified for them now than before. For example, this past Diwali my family celebrated in proper style complete with a pooja, a grand feast, lighting diyas and fireworks. On my own in the tiny town of Ithaca, I chose to meet a few friends for dinner at a Vietnamese restaurant, then stopped by at a bar to sing some karaoke. I didn't drink out of respect to the holiday, but I also did not go out of my way to celebrate. In a few years, I don't know whether or not I'll have this same lax attitude towards religious practices. While I'd like to pass on certain traditions to my own children one day, I worry that I will become as dogmatic as the generation before me. Arriving at my current understanding of self, religion, and obedience was certainly a challenge, but even more so will be learning how to teach this awareness and balance in the future.

Someday Never Comes

Rajpreet Heir

That afternoon in Asheville, North Carolina, even the slopes we passed on our drive to the Biltmore Estate, the largest home in America, seemed to own a sort of troubled stillness. Tension was there in the hushed early April sun and stares from residents.

My twin brother, Manvir, and our parents didn't seem to be affected, especially since we were finally done with college campus tours. But even while visiting Duke, Davidson, and Wake Forest a few days earlier on our spring break trip, I'd felt uneasy. Maybe it was because the warmth meant the conclusion of high school indoor track practices back home in Indianapolis – no more crunches and easy baton hand-off drills; instead we would be running 900 meter repeats and time trials for outdoor track. Or maybe something else was pinching at my excitement.

It all seemed too good to be true. No woman in my family had ever lived away from home for school. My grandmothers were from rural Punjab farming villages and didn't get to finish middle school. Born in England, my mom was the first to attend college in her whole family, but she'd lived at home while getting her degree and finished it in Indiana while raising us. Despite the little academic encouragement she'd received, she regularly took us to the library until we could drive ourselves, found camps for us every summer, attended our games and award ceremonies, and made sure she was home to hear about our school days when we got off the bus. I was the first-born granddaughter on both sides of my family and I'd had the most privileged education of all my female relatives. Still, I was only tentatively imagining myself on the college campuses we visited.

We started touring schools when our brother, Jaskaran, was a sophomore and we were freshmen. As a family, we went to Notre Dame, Vanderbilt, and Wash. U. Neither of my parents were taken on trips like that while growing up in England. My mom's parents didn't even take her to a restaurant once in the twenty-two years she lived there. When my dad's family moved to Indianapolis in 1977, when he was fourteen, his parents had bigger concerns than taking their kids to the other side of the country for campus visits. After graduating from college, my dad visited England for the first time since he'd left, and on the trip, his relatives instructed him to meet with some Indian families to find a wife. He did as he was told and agreed to marry my mom. Both families had similar values and approved of each other. My parents didn't complain or speak back to their parents. They just did as they were told.

I can't remember exactly why we visited North Carolina specifically that break – maybe because the track coaches at some of the schools had been interested in Manvir. Other students at our private high school were also touring campuses, making it seem like the next step in the college search. Several got into Ivies each year, and each year, students, parents, teachers, and administrators contributed to a high-pressure admissions process. My brothers and I put extra pressure on ourselves all four years because we recognized the sacrifices our parents made to send us to a fancy high school and we tried to imitate their tireless work ethic. Yet, there was something unspoken among us that was beginning to make me wonder if I'd actually get to join my classmates or even my twin as they packed up their suitcases and got on flights to attend colleges in distant cities. Having surface-level thoughts about the whole matter seemed to be the best plan, so I focused on taking the Biltmore trip for what it was: a break for all of us at the end of a week away.

What happened was, I flirted with a strange blond man in the Biltmore gift store. After the hour-long drive back to the house we were renting, my mom announced she was on strike and sat down on the couch in the front room. She made almost all of our meals every single day of the week, so the occasional strike made a lot of sense. Manvir joined her. My dad started to make the dinner and I disappeared into my room, which was only a few feet from the kitchen, to write about the day.

I'd fixated all afternoon on the blond man. He'd dressed like a rock star in sunglasses and tight jeans and my dad had even wondered if he was Roger Daltrey. When I finally got the chance to leave my parents and approach the blond man, two things happened: I realized he was much older and less attractive than I'd thought, and my mom dragged me away within a few minutes. What I'd done was bold and out of character. In that moment, I should have felt victorious. I had been a daring, forward woman. I had achieved the goal I had been working toward all afternoon. But with my mom leading me away from him, I had felt lower than I had the whole trip. As we'd left the Biltmore, my dad made an off-hand comment about how dumb I'd been to start asking a stranger questions, but nothing else had happened. Yet, I could sense punishment of some sort coming my way.

From the kitchen, my dad slammed the fridge door shut, and I knew what would happen next: the same thing that happened anytime my mom went on a trip, or when older relatives were over and my dad wanted to impress them. I had to become domestic.

"Come help me make scrambled eggs," he told me.

"No, I don't want to," I called out from my room, pulling the covers over myself in the twin bed. The wool comforter was hideous and there was a large mallard duck on the front. Scrambled eggs were actually one of my favorite meals and I enjoyed making them, but I hated it when my dad insisted I help him. He rarely asked the boys to help around the house, but I still had to rake leaves and pick up sticks.

The Biltmore should have been the perfect outing since it was an American success story come to life. My dad had been selling vacuum cleaners door-to-door since he was fifteen and entrepreneurial accomplishments resonated with him. Growing up, he was always hustling, looking for ways to make money and help his family. Like my mom, he was also the first person in his entire family to attend college. The impressiveness of the Estate appealed to all of us, but especially him.

In my room, I put on headphones to listen to the same song I'd been playing since we'd arrived in North Carolina: "Someday Never Comes" by Creedence Clearwater Revival. I'd added it to my iPod shuffle by mistake, but couldn't stop listening to it, perhaps because the song made me feel close to my dad and reminded me of the things I liked about him. The gap between us seemed to grow every year and felt especially apparent on that spring break trip, with my departure from high school and home next year more in sight than ever. Though my relationship with my dad had become challenging after I entered womanhood, as it does for many daughters, we still connected when he would drive me places and teach me about the greatest music he'd encountered in his lifetime, like CCR.

He was still asking for me, so I took out my headphones to listen. "Get up and burn a frickin' calorie," he said, temper rising. But I didn't want to serve anyone; I didn't want to make my dad approve of me for the wrong reasons.

"Get your ass in here," he said. He didn't talk to my brothers that way. I got up and locked the door so he wouldn't see me cry. Jumping to cusswords wasn't a usual thing, but the Biltmore incident and the fear and anger he must have felt at seeing me act out seemed to make him more heated.

Though raised in England, both of my parents seemed inclined to hang on to old-time values. Even across two different western continents, our ancestors' influence was real in my life. It was as if the threat of western thinking had made them clench their views even tighter. Women had been treated a certain way for generations, and suddenly there I was defying what they knew. My parents and their parents had done what was expected of them and why shouldn't I?

My dad banged on my bedroom door and shook the doorknob. I pulled the blanket closer, hugged my pillow, and looked at the splintered wall next to my bed. There was no mirror in the room; I wouldn't be able to see if there was any evidence of crying. Other girls would at least have their makeup compacts, but I wasn't allowed to have one.

"I'll help," I heard Manvir say.

But then, my mom decided Manvir should get a run in at a track before it got too dark and we should all come too. He hadn't gotten a chance to run the whole week. There were chances on other days, but my mom refused to let him run alone in a city she didn't know well. A track would allow her to keep him in sight. My dad stopped getting the eggs ready since the rental van was registered in his name and only he could drive it. I knew they weren't going to let me stay behind. By that age, I'd given up trying to fight my mom when she wanted us to do a family activity. Maybe her forcefulness came from her own sadness that she was an ocean away from her parents and siblings.

My mother knocked on the door, calling my name. When I opened it, she said, "Get out, we're all going to the track and you can't stay here." Sometimes, my mom comforted me when my dad yelled at me, but this time, she sounded exhausted with my behavior. After wiping my face and nose, I left the room. We all got into the van and stared out of our own windows.

૭

We went to a local track that was at the bottom of some hills. The sunken position of the field allowed for naturally raised bleachers. Red spray-painted bushes on the hillside spelled AHS. Because the stadium lights weren't on, we weren't going to be able to stay long. I knew I should run too, but also knew I needed to do more than run to fix why I was slower than my brother. I decided to just walk laps around the track with my parents.

Manvir was older than me by seven minutes. I came out backwards and peeing. The only hair I had was a unibrow. I had jaundice too and had to stay at the hospital for a few days under a lamp. I liked to think those days are the reason why I have always been behind Manvir. Earlier that semester, Jaskaran asked our US History teacher how Manvir and I were doing in his class and the teacher told him, "Rajpreet tries hard, but Manvir is just the better student." During sophomore year I tried convincing myself and my mom that I had dyslexia, but after taking several tests with the middle school counselor, the results showed nothing unordinary in my learning abilities, which was unfortunate because I had grown attached to the list of dyslexic celebrities.

At the track, my shoes wouldn't stay on my feet and I set them to the side by the starting line. I was wearing a tank top under a pink jacket my aunt in England gave me. My mom said the tank was too low at first but I wore it so many times in the past month that she gave up – a rare victory. I tried wearing lip-gloss as eye shadow for a while but she noticed one morning in the van when I looked down at my backpack before getting out. Elizabeth, my first white friend with a home situation like mine, bought brown fishnets for us and we wore them under our jeans on Fridays. If you looked closely at our thighs when we were seated, the ridges of the tights were visible under the denim.

It was our second lap around as we were nearing the two-hundred meter start when my parents began.

"Do you even know why you want to go to Wake Forest? You say a different major at every school we visit," my dad said.

"I like law or architecture," I replied. But I knew where this was leading.

"These schools are expensive; they cost more than our house. And we're not going to get any financial aid even though we will have three kids in private colleges. They want us to spend our retirement money," my mom said.

I knew I couldn't tell them I felt something magical at Wake Forest. I wanted to have deep discussions about life in the lobby of the languages building. I wanted to toilet paper the trees and make it look as if it had snowed like in the picture from the brochure. I didn't know what a Demon Deacon was, but I wanted to be one.

"I'll work really hard," I said.

"Why should we pay for you to go somewhere if you can't even help your dad make scrambled eggs?" my mom asked.

Manvir passed us with a flick of a wave, his long bony legs in short shorts. He was on the inside lane. His face was smooth and the impact of the track caused the skin around his jaw to bounce slightly. If I were a boy that's what I'd look like, moving fast with a matter-of-fact foot-fall. I should have been the boy. My mustache came in before Manvir's.

"There's no airport near Wake Forest. You'd have to get a ride every time," she said.

"We can ask Peter how he does it once we get back home," I replied. Peter, Jaskaran's friend from the year above, had just been accepted into Wake Forest and lived half an hour away from us in Indianapolis.

"All liberal arts schools are the same. When we get back we're going to the Preview Day at DePauw," she said.

In my mind, DePauw, which was only an hour away from home, was beneath me. Anyone from my school could get into DePauw. In high school, I had started at the bottom of our class, coming from a public school system and not knowing how to type fast enough to finish in-class essays, but I had slowly caught up and then risen to the top quarter. For a long time, school had been my obsession. There were no parties, drinking, or boys, or spring break trips with friends. Other people at my school who worked as hard were going to Vanderbilt, Columbia, and Emory. The least my parents could do, I believed, was to send me to Wake Forest in Winston-Salem, North Carolina.

Any college in Indiana, I was sure, was too close to home. I was too young to think about how it wasn't always what university you went to, but what you made of it, or to understand that going to college was a privilege. For me especially, it was a privilege given the lack of educational opportunities for my female relatives of previous generations. Still, I compared myself not with them, but with my brothers.

"But Jaskaran gets to leave Indiana and Manvir will, too," I whined, knowing that my parents were going to get even madder. We had just learned Jaskaran got into the University of Pennsylvania Wharton School. Jaskaran was on spring break in Florida, staying in a house with his friends – both male *and* female. My mind didn't even dare dream of such trips. I had long since accepted my parents' restrictions on my social interactions.

"That's because they are doing business programs. You don't know what you're doing. Manvir wants to run and there aren't good enough programs in

Indiana," my mom said. I had no way of defending myself. Their argument made sense. How could I be made out of the same stuff as my brothers and be so stupid? I was the errant ball from my family's playing field.

"You need to be realistic here," my dad said. We had circled back around again.

"Why should we send you away? How do you think it feels when you go talking to strange men? You scared us," my mom said, referring to the blond man at the Biltmore.

"What the hell were you thinking? Don't be stupid. Come on," my dad said. He was angry, hands in his leather jacket pockets, head down as he marched on.

My throat muscles seemed to bulge in an effort not to cry.

"Why would you do that to us? He could have taken you. You need to use your common sense," my mom was saying, her voice peaking. If I was capable of flirting with a grown man in my parents' presence, they worried about what else I might do when away from them, regularly surrounded by boys in co-ed dorms and at frat parties. They wouldn't be able to protect me then and this scared them. Speaking to a stranger hadn't been smart and part of me knew that.

Right then, though, I focused on how I hated my mom's worn pink corduroy jacket and small rhinestone hoop earrings. She could have been wearing something that actually showed her amazing figure and she could have been wearing jewelry that was as artful and interesting as she was. She rarely bought stuff for herself. She was always stressing sacrifice, appreciation, thank you letters, and sticking to family values.

I stared at the metal fence near the road and wondered if I could just take off, leap over the fence, roll down the slope, and live in North Carolina for good. I would wear halter-tops and be fast in something other than running. I would actually be able to take pride in my body, speak loudly, and leave the house on my own without having to ask for permission.

"Okay," I said. I spoke in a gargled voice, relying on my practiced discipline to keep my emotions in check. In my fantasy, I wanted to start running. Sprinting with no hair tie, pumping my fists and growling. Maybe I'd finally get a personal record in something and make my coaches proud. I'd give one lap with all the hope winding out of my body and they would tap their clipboards and say, "It's about time."

"You've been acting really ungrateful," my mom was saying. My socks weren't providing enough protection now from the asphalt track. My heels hurt.

I stared at the big number two in my lane as we closed in on the end-zone. Unlike my brother, I knew I would never get to have waffles with a pressed WF seal at the eight-dollar weekend buffet that student athletes loved.

The whole North Carolina trip, I began to suspect, had been a setup. My parents had been waiting for me to slip and be wild, so they could have a reason to keep me from leaving. No drinking, no kissing, no smoking, no dancing with boys, no Bs, no two-piece swim suits, no makeup, no thongs, no strapless dresses, no driver's license. But they still sensed falseness in me.

My mom and her mom and my dad's mom were also watched closely by their families in their time. We may have been in a different country, but all of it was old news. The food, movies, dress, music, and language, were left behind in moving to new countries, but the rules for girls mostly stayed the same.

Manvir passed us again – shirtless now. He was trying to break the four by eight record. I knew he would do it. His relay team might make it to Regionals. In contrast, I would be lucky to be an alternate for the four by one. Most likely, I wouldn't even get that.

The long-distance coach would tell me I must have running somewhere in my genes too since Manvir could run so well. When I ran, though, it was like I was some transparent ghost. I was not all there. It was someone else on the track with aimless strides and a cornered expression trying to catch up to her brothers, or her teammates, or her parents' expectations, or the strong independent woman she longed to become. Running with purpose meant disturbing my family's structure. My brothers didn't seem to have this same internal conflict and they were gaining laps on me in most areas. Closing that gap seemed more and more discouraging, yet I didn't want them to slow down on my behalf either. My parents' enthusiasm for their academic and athletic performances was greater than it was for me; it was nice if I ran well and got good grades, but nicer, from their perspective, if I was a good Indian daughter and stayed close to home for school.

Around we went again. I avoided eye contact with my parents as we passed the bleachers, scoreboard, stadium light poles, long jump pit, and starting line once more. The track looked like tracks always looked, like a contained space that wasn't going to help me. My heartbeat was steady and didn't really seem to be mine. The rest of my body didn't seem to belong to me either. A sort of silence slowly filled me. I knew I was going to be quiet for a long time.

Affording the Perfect Family

Leila Khan

The Excel spreadsheet makes it clear: we can't afford a second child. I play with the numbers again, calculating optimistic tax returns and a bigger bonus, but when I click on the sum total icon, the number still is not enough. I have done this exercise too many times to doubt the hard truth of the numbers. I close my five-year old MacBook and lay my head down on the smooth white surface.

How did we get here? I am a forty-year-old professional married to another professional. We both work. I am an attorney for the federal government and my husband trades bonds for a regional bank. Why is having a second child such a financial stretch for us?

I reopen my laptop and sign in to Facebook. I scroll through the pages of girls who are family friends, Desi girls I grew up with in Orange County, girls who married neurosurgeons, cardiologists, and radiologists, and who post pictures of themselves with their two or three children. My stomach and chest tighten. A golf ball sits in my throat. I shut my laptop again.

My family immigrated to the United States when I was ten years old. We came from Pakistan via Singapore, Malaysia, the United Kingdom, and France. My dad worked for an international bank and my mother managed a household of three kids in constant geographic upheaval.

For my parents, as with most South Asian parents, financial security and upward social mobility for their children are major preoccupations. For their daughters, they usually see two paths to prosperity: 1) marrying a doctor or 2) becoming a doctor. Since pathway two is seen as too much work and as consuming important child-bearing years, most parents, including mine, focus on pathway one: the doctor son-in-law.

My mother started fantasizing about my married life when my father lost his job with the bank and I got my period. She really wanted me to have what she didn't: the doctor husband who would provide financial security. Her constant diet of Bollywood films and family gossip fueled her fantasies. She imagined a grand wedding, an opulent home, and a leisurely lifestyle, none of which she felt she had.

"Leila!" She charged into my room with the cordless phone in her hand. I looked up from my chemistry homework with sleepy eyes. "I just got off the phone with Noora auntie. She said that there is a very nice doctor in Fresno who is looking for a wife. He says he wants a girl with *colored* eyes. I told Noora auntie to tell them about you. Even though you don't have *colored* eyes, you have very nice eyes. They are almost light brown, nahn?"

I rolled my *very nice* eyes. "Ma, if the guy's criteria for a wife is colored eyes, then he sounds like a jerk and I wouldn't want to marry him."

"But, Leila jaan, he's a *doctor.*"

∾

Much to my parents' disappointment, I neither became nor married a doctor. My own dreams of becoming a doctor dissolved as I struggled through high school chemistry and biology. I didn't have the right brains for this road. As for marrying a doctor, I didn't achieve the right mix of beauty, docility, and "good fortune" to secure the doctor husband.

The truth is, I was looking at a different path, one that did not necessarily end with money and status. I was looking for adventure, romance, and independence. I spent a year studying Arabic in Tunisia, worked for the UN in war-torn Bosnia, dated an Italian man from Milano for three years, and traveled around India by myself for a month. I found all that I was looking for – along with severe parental disapproval and periods of estrangement, heartbreak, and a whole lot of financial insecurity. My Italian boyfriend and I had a devastating breakup on the eve of my relocation to Europe to live with him. I had racked up student loans in excess of $100,000. At 34, after a layoff, I found myself single and unemployed.

I often wonder what my life would have been like if I had followed the doctor-husband path. What if I had obeyed my parents and married someone they had carefully selected? The promise of that life taunts me these days as I feel my own position in the middle class slipping. Student loans, mortgage payments, property taxes, the cost of childcare, saving for retirement, saving for the kid's college fund, the bills pile up and each month I return to that Excel spreadsheet, worrying about how and when we will be able to stay ahead of the spending curve.

I tell myself I'm not alone in my worries, that I'm not a failure, that my experience actually is part of a much larger phenomenon. After all, the decline of the middle class in America is widely reported and studied. Last year, an article on CNN Money.com reported that the number of people who identified themselves as lower class had soared.[1] An opinion piece on Forbes.com said that our economy was taking a dumbbell shape with most of the jobs on either end of the income spectrum and few jobs left in the middle.[2]

President Obama says we need "middle-class economics." During a recent speech to students at Kansas University, he explained:

> And so part of what we have to do is to make sure that we're giving families *some sense of security in the midst of all this change*. And that means helping folks *afford childcare*. It means helping folks *afford college*. It means helping folks get *paid leave at work*. It means making sure people have *health care*. It means helping the *first-time homebuyer*. It means helping folks save for *retirement*. . .[3]

My shame subsides. I nod vigorously as he speaks. Yes, Mr. President, yes, that's exactly what we have to do. Not just for ourselves, but for our children, too.

৵৹

My mother tucks her white dupatta behind her ear as she stirs the onions and spices in the pan. The aroma of frying onions, ginger, garlic, cumin, and chili powder rises through the kitchen and adjacent family room. The chicken pieces sizzle as they hit the pan and the fragrance intensifies.

I have settled down to read *Peter Rabbit* with my two-year old daughter on the sofa. My mother is visiting for a week and enjoys preparing dinner for the family. She prefers her chicken curry and basmati rice to our quinoa and black beans with salsa or leek soup. This arrangement works well for me as I can relax with my daughter when I get home from work instead of racing around the kitchen throwing random beans, grains, and vegetables together.

My mother calls out from the kitchen, "You have to eat more meat, Leila. It'll give you strength. You look so tired and weak all the time. You'll need more strength to have a little brother for our Eva jaanu." She talks about how she is always praying for her next grandchild, hopefully a grandson, she adds.

I want to share the burden of my Excel spreadsheet with her, but something holds me back. *The American Dream* – that's what silences me. The idea that each successive generation does better than its predecessor. My parents were able to raise three children on one income. My father retired at 62 and my parents are living off the income of their rental properties. They achieved not only the *American Dream*, but the immigrant version of it, too.

Not me.

⁓

I now understand those South Asian parental preoccupations. Mapping our child's future with two paths to financial security is much easier than fighting for middle-class economics. As a working mom of a young child, I'm too tired to work for meaningful change. I'm just trying to get through each day without losing my temper. So I write small checks to organizations that try to actualize President Obama's economic agenda, practice gratitude, and avoid thinking about doctors.

When I look at my skinny, almost three-year-old with her large brown eyes and stick straight brown hair, an intense desire to protect her spreads through me. I yearn to give her a sibling.

A few months ago, as I was driving her to preschool, she said, "Mama, I have a brother."

"Aaah, is that right?" I looked at her in the rearview mirror. "What is his name?"

"Kaio."

"Kaio? That's a nice name."

"Yes, I'm a big sister."

I didn't know what to say.

For a few weeks she talked about her brother and how she was a big sister. I knew she was imitating a few of her classmates at preschool who had younger brothers. I let her imagination run.

One afternoon, when I picked her up from preschool, she said, "Mama, Scarlett told me I wasn't a big sister." I kneeled down to meet her gaze. Her eyes searched mine. I wrapped her in my arms and hugged her.

"You are a big sister," I said into her hair. "You're a big sister to your bear, panda, tiger, and all the other toys you sleep with at night."

How did we get here?

I know what you're thinking. *Surely she can't let money drive this decision. People do it on much less and seem happy.* I agree with you and I realize this. What I'm saying is that it hurts to be in this place after attending a good law school, borrowing $147,000 to pay for my education, working as a lawyer for twelve years, getting most of my school loan paid off by the time our child came, and still feeling financially insecure. It's a swamp of self-doubt. I can't help but wonder if my parents had been right all along.

Policymakers talk about the need for affordable childcare. In the Bay Area, the average cost of full-time, good childcare for two very young children – say, an infant and a toddler – is over $3,000 a month. Live-in help may cost less, but it presupposes a spare bedroom, which is a luxury in the Bay Area. The cost of childcare goes down as the children grow older and then, if they attend a public school, the cost is significantly less. The cost of childcare does not include money spent on diapers, formula, food, clothes, strollers, cribs, security gates, and the occasional babysitter for a desperately needed date-night.

Sociologist Marianne Cooper writes about the anxiety affecting all families in the US, an anxiety caused by the lack of financial security and the threadbare safety net.[4] She describes the various emotional responses people deploy to cope with their fears and worries, such as compartmentalizing, letting one spouse do all the worrying, fixating, and turning to God. Her research reassures me. I'm not alone. I didn't make bad decisions.

At night, while listening to meditation apps on my iPhone, I realize the importance of coping with these fears and worries in ways that do not alienate my husband or hurt my child. Even though Cooper finds that one spouse in the marriage usually does most of the worrying and that spouse usually is the woman, she also notes the marital angst caused by carrying this weight.

So what are these non-destructive ways of coping? Especially when you have a monkey on your back screeching, *could have been different, could have been better, could have been safer.* Cooper's book offers no solutions for managing the emotions that result from economic insecurity.

While I sometimes feel like the "practice gratitude" manifesto has become too commercial (it's on *shopping bags* for god's sake), the research confirms its unquestionable value in improving mental health. Dr. Robert Emmons, the world's leading scientific expert on gratitude, says that cultivating gratitude produces physical, psychological, and social benefits.[5] Specifically, it wards off negative and toxic emotions like envy and regret.

I keep returning to gratitude as the way to stay sane. I focus on our health, our jobs, and this beautiful part of the world in which we live. I remind myself of my husband's integrity, tremendous work ethic, and devotion to our daughter. Each night, after I sing her off-key bedtime lullabies in the dark, he comes into her room with a flashlight, creating a camp-like atmosphere, and they read stories together for nearly an hour. I think about the way my daughter shrieks with glee and races towards me when she sees me arrive at her preschool. There is reliability, steadiness, and moments of unparalleled joy here.

I may not have everything I want, but I must cherish what I do.

Endnotes

1. http://economy.money.cnn.com/2014/01/28/middle-class/
2. http://www.forbes.com/sites/jeffreydorfman/2014/06/07/middle-class-jobs-are-disappearing-and-the-fed-is-the-culprit/
3. http://www.whitehouse.gov/the-press-office/2015/01/22/remarks-president-middle-class-economics-university-kansas-lawrence-ks
4. Cooper, Marianne, *Cut Adrift: Families in Insecure Times*, University of California Press, 2014.
5. http://greatergood.berkeley.edu/article/item/why_gratitude_is_good

Acting the Part

Rachna Khatau

Waiting backstage at a small black box theatre in Chicago, I was so nervous I could feel my heartbeat in my throat – I still hadn't fully beaten my stage fright. It was opening night, and my parents were two of only a handful of audience members who had come to see the play. The theatre was tiny, and, oh yeah, I wasn't getting paid. But at the end of the performance, my parents jumped to their feet and started a standing ovation. They always start a standing ovation.

There are countless stories like this from my childhood through my career. My parents, along with my sister, have flown and driven around the country to rally around me as I studied, competed, and performed. My family is the very definition of an awe-inspiring support system.

The beginning of my career in the arts was bumpy, to say the least. I had been dancing around the front yard for days, excited for my big acting debut in a play hosted by our local park district. I hadn't, however, managed to learn one key element necessary to perform: My line. My one line. I was five years old. When the time came for me to step forward and recite my line, I froze. Finally, another girl in the play came up and whispered *my* line in my ear. I summoned the courage to deliver the line and promptly forgot it again. Yes, someone *told* me my line, and I still couldn't do it.

My parents later told me that was the moment they thought, "Okay, she's not a performer." But I was, and I am. My park district performance was the first in a series of events that solidified for me that performing was, in fact, my calling. And when I made my dream clear to my family, they were all in.

During my senior year of high school, I auditioned to be in a girl group. A female N*SYNC, if you will. As soon as I got home from the audition, the phone rang. I had been chosen to be in the group. I was thrilled – and terrified. It was the first day of a two-year journey that launched my family into a world of contracts, attorneys, and recording studios. It meant traveling to other cities to rehearse and perform without my parents ... *and not going to college*. But my parents didn't flinch. An opportunity had presented itself for me to do what I wanted to do, and they were letting me do it. My Indian, built-everything-they-have-from-scratch, traditional-career-oriented parents not only *let* me not go to college, they were thrilled that I wasn't going to college. They welcomed the experience I would gain having the chance to train, travel, and work as a singer.

My parents were turning negatively depicted South Asian parenting clichés upside down. They may not have known much about performance arts, but, ironically, they were taking the skills they did have and applying them in positive ways to work in my favor. My parents' support for me wasn't as simple as, "Oh, you love the arts? Go be artistic!" From their Indian and immigrant upbringing, they knew it would take hard work and dedication. So, while my parents let me choose my own path, they pushed me to make sure I created for myself the best chance for success. Their attitude was: if you're serious about this, you have to work harder at it than you've ever worked at anything. Push yourself every day and never give up. Instead of fearing the unknown, they were trying to give me structure in an industry where there is no structure, no rubric for success. So, they helped me create a rubric for myself. I have pursued my career with their unyielding support, and I would not be living my dreams without them.

And yet, because I am Indian, there is an underlying assumption among most people I meet that my parents are not okay with me pursuing the arts, that they don't understand it, that they are embarrassed or ashamed, that they wish I had become a doctor or a lawyer or an engineer. Lucky for me, these assumptions are wrong. Yes, there are serious challenges that come with being in the arts. For my parents, not having any insight or connections and the helplessness they felt as a result has definitely led to some frustration and confusion over the years. But the challenge for them has never been supporting me, and that surprises people.

One year at a friend's Diwali party, an Indian aunty asked me if I was a doctor, like the host. "No," I said. "I'm an actor." "Oh," she replied. "But what do you do?" I tried not to react as I repeated, "I'm an actor. I'm a full-time actor." Her question didn't feel like a judgment so much as it did sincere confusion, and, in that moment, I realized that her response to me had not meant to be malicious. It was true bewilderment – she had simply never before in her life spoken to an Indian woman who was seriously pursuing acting. In fact, that is the overwhelming response I get from most uncles and aunties in our Indian community, and I don't blame them for their ignorance.

It's a slightly different story, however, with younger people in my community. Indian Americans my age who have questioned my relationship with my parents because of my career. They are the ones who seem confused by (and sometimes judgmental of) what I do. Time and time again I've been told, "My parents would never let me do that."

My response to that is: Why? And how can you be certain? Sometimes I feel Indian aunties and uncles get the short end of the stick – how can we, as an entire generation of young Indian Americans, be so sure of how our parents will react to us if we never even give them a chance?

But young Indian Americans constantly assert that getting support from their parents for a career like mine would be out of the question. They ask me questions like, "How long are you going to do this?" and "What's your backup plan?" When those questions come up, I try to explain that this is not a phase or a trial – it is my career, and I will do it as long as I'm able. Then the inevitable follow-up question is, "Are your parents *okay* with that?" As if "okay" is the highest level of acceptance Indian parents can muster for a child who has chosen the arts.

I try to explain how supportive my parents have been and sometimes try to hint that if they gave their own parents a chance, they might be surprised. But Indian Americans of my generation are flabbergasted when they hear that my parents are supportive and even encouraging of my career. Didn't they want me to become a doctor or engineer? Aren't they horrified by the prospect of me having to (gasp!) kiss someone on stage? Oh, the scandal!

The thing I'm most struck by in these conversations is that none of these people – my peers, my supposed community – none of them has ever asked me the *real* questions. Did *I* want to become a doctor or engineer? Am *I* horrified by the prospect of kissing someone on stage? The only people who *have* asked me those questions are my parents.

To be truthful, one of my main concerns is how *they* will deal with my decisions. Not they themselves, but how they will deal with the reactions of others to my decisions. My parents have always assured me that they don't care what others think or say when it comes to my career. They can handle the occasional mustachioed uncle who has watched too many Bollywood movies when he declares, "I would never let my daughter do [fill in the blank]!" They believe that people who truly know me will support my choices, champion my success, and empathize with my failures.

Once I learned that both my parents and I could navigate these assumptions *within* our community, I realized that there was another battle to be fought. It turns out that even most non-Indians I meet are certain that my parents loathe my career. They assume that my parents and I have a strained relationship. Either my story really is an anomaly, or the stereotype that we as a community have managed to paint and perpetuate – the image of academic honors and financial success as the measures by which Indian parents judge and relate to their children – truly is monolithic.

One of the most ridiculous assumptions from non-Indians about my relationship with my parents is that because I'm an actor, I'm "not that Indian." That I must want to distance myself from the oppressive culture whence I came. That's a tough one for me. I'm a hard-working person with strong morals and loving ties to my culture and heritage. I've always enjoyed celebrating my ethnicity and religion. I am an American, but I am also Indian, and I happen to be a performer. It is saddening to me that, based solely on my choice of career, people would believe that I am disinterested or dismissive of my Indian identity, and therefore, of my parents. To be clear, I most certainly am not. Being brown, being Indian, doesn't mean that's all I am. Just like being an actor doesn't mean I am not, in fact, a proud Indian woman.

All of this raises an interesting question. What if my parents had done this stereotypical thing and forced me down a different path? What if they had discouraged me from following my dreams? Well, my career definitely would have been different had my parents not been supportive. I might not have overcome the obstacles that allow me to perform; I might not have found my voice (literally and figuratively); I might not have found my confidence; and I might not have found a way to be okay with "failing." Failure and success don't always have concrete measures, and in an industry like show business, that can destroy you. If my parents had not supported me, the near misses would have likely felt like failures. But with their support, I am able to see each of those moments as more than just stepping-stones – I see them as wins.

If my family sounds too good to be true, trust me, I know. No one's life is all sunshine and rainbows, and mine hasn't been either. But when it comes to my career, I have had a different experience than the imagination of my community allows for.

So what kind of parent do I want to be to my (thus far non-existent) kids? Aside from the usual requests that any future children be healthy, happy, and kind, I wish for them structure and stability. A part of me hopes they don't want to want to be artists, not because I'll be an Indian mom trying to push them down a more "traditional" path, but because I am an artist, and I know how heart-wrenching it can be. I hope their dreams are easier to follow because, like my parents wanted for me, I want them to achieve their goals and live their dreams. But whatever they choose, I will try to live up to the example my parents set with me. My road has been long and winding, but I am a working actor. And that would not have happened had my parents not been along for the ride.

Becoming a Reluctant Breadwinner

Swati Khurana

I. Breadwinner

I imagine that word in all capitals, outlined in yellow, against a red background – the graphics befitting a superhero. As a child, I never actually played princess or imagined myself being rescued. Take a summer afternoon in 1981, when I was fearless, in a Wonder Woman bathing suit over my six-year-old frame, lanky, knobby, and hirsute. My sister was a year old. She was toddling, squatting, tipping over. We had a pool, with a perimeter of concrete, and then a garden to the side. My grandmother was gardening and watching my sister toddle. I was on the swing set.

Then I heard a scream unlike any I had heard. It was my grandmother. My baby sister had fallen in the pool. My grandmother, who had just arrived from India with all of us a few years ago, didn't know how to swim. I leapt off the swing set, ran past the pear tree, and jumped into the pool. I had been taking lessons, but I hadn't learned to swim in the deep end yet. I jumped in, pulled her up, and handed her to my grandmother. My mother heard the commotion and ran outside. My sister coughed out water, but she was fine.

When I try to summon my bravery and resolve, I remember that moment of being a superhero. It's also my creation story of my own feminism – feeling that I could summon the strength to do anything. When I hear about women being able to lift up cars for their babies, I feel as if I have first-hand experience at doing what seems physically impossible when a baby's life is at stake.

Decades later, when my two-month paid maternity leave ended, I returned to work full-time. My husband was leaving his sales-based career and was in the process of going back to university to become a school teacher – decisions we made together. I had the flexibility to be full- or part-time and the job security to go back to work later. But we couldn't afford that.

When I was pregnant, this plan to return to work was abstract. Soon, I realized I was the breadwinner and had transformed into neither the mother I grew up with nor the one I expected to be. I had a baby girl, a husband, and a stepdaughter, a job that was fulfilling with a degree of flexibility, the ability to provide for my family while pursuing my creative work, and yet, I felt like a failure.

I failed because I missed too many moments, including my daughter's first steps, which were recorded on her babysitter's cell phone and sent to me. I actually missed the video message for an hour because I was in a meeting. I missed seeing these steps in person for three days because I left the house before she woke up and came home after she fell asleep. On the fourth day of her walking, when I could take a day off, I finally saw her steps for myself. I beamed, but I also wondered, what else would I miss?

II. Becoming

I was born in India, raised Punjabi/Hindu, in Poughkeepsie, NY, by a (mostly) stay-at-home mother and grandmother, and a physician father. My husband is Puerto Rican, born and raised in the Bronx, by a father in the civil service and a mother who worked part-time and was often at home. We both grew up in patriarchal households in different patriarchal societies – Indian, Puerto Rican, American. We are also both feminists. And yet, our new life together was a major adjustment.

When I was in my first trimester, my husband and I got married. When I met my husband, I had already been married and divorced, had a great teaching job and art career, and had been living in a cute two-bedroom apartment I had bought as a single, divorced woman in Brooklyn. I had a very grown up life for over a decade before I announced to my Indian parents that I was pregnant. They were excited to have a grandchild and had come to see my boyfriend as family. We had been together for a few years, would have likely gotten engaged, married, and tried to have a family in a more traditional – even obedient – order, had I not been unexpectedly pregnant.

My parents were thrilled to welcome their first grandchild, and they happily called the extended family to tell them I was pregnant and to invite them to a party they threw as a wedding reception. One may think that announcing an unplanned pregnancy as a single – technically divorced woman – would create conflict with one's Indian parents. In my case, it did not. Partially, the thrill and surprise was that for a long time becoming a mother had been impossible for me.

For a set of circumstances that were partially physical, psychological, emotional, and relational, I was not able to consummate my first marriage at age 22. I suffered from vaginismus – a condition that made intercourse, and hence pregnancy, impossible. When I told my parents, on the cusp of my divorce, they embraced my confession and vowed to support my treatment. After years of psychotherapy and a year of physical therapy, I was "cured." With my mother, I was frank, sharing details about the dildos I had to use in physical therapy, the anti-anxiety medication I had to take for pelvic exams, and the pain and shame I felt. I told her that if I ever married again, I would not delay sexual intimacy, and, in fact, ensure that in addition to emotional, intellectual, and political compatibility – we were also compatible sexually.

My difficult journey – both emotionally and physically – to become a mother is critical in understanding my despair about the kind of mother I was becoming after I had my baby. Before I had my child, I had tried to tell myself that this desire for motherhood was not that large and aching and that I could be fulfilled with a wonderful circle of friends, exciting travels, and an artistic practice. And that remains true (I resent the societal pressure on women to feel incomplete without becoming mothers). But in my case, I used to weep every Mother's Day because it reminded me of my aching desire.

So when I finally had a baby, the pain of not having the option to be the kind of mother I had always wanted to be (devoted, attentive, ever-present), was heartbreaking.

III. Reluctant

It shouldn't have been so hard to embrace the role of the breadwinner, but it was. On the outside, it seemed like an easy feminist proposition. On the inside, I felt incredible difficulty coming to terms with my own decisions. When I imagined having a baby, I pictured leisurely days of snuggling, breast-feeding, and going to cafés with my child. Should I have delayed having a child until I had saved more money to take more paid leave? Should I have only looked at male partners who would be "good providers" so that I could have the option to not work, to be at home as a mother, to make art without worrying about a paying gig? But the reality was, I was never attracted to someone just because I envisioned their "taking care of me." Instead, I was attracted to men who could cook and would cook for me, men who saw "taking care" of someone as not just being through breadwinning but also through the domestic acts of care. One of my earliest dates with my husband was when he visited me when I was sick. He bought groceries and made me soup.

And yet, I felt like a failure because I couldn't be at home with my newborn for longer than I was. Having incredible difficulty with breastfeeding amplified my own grief around not being the mother I would have liked to be. I felt the double pressures of both college-educated, middle-class America to be the most ecologically-minded, attached parent and my own Indian upbringing which encouraged a different kind of self-sacrifice for a child. Even some of the most fierce and inspiring Indian feminists and artists I knew either had husbands who were breadwinners or had fewer financial pressures than I had. In my mind, they could do their work and still feel like mothers.

Instead of an Indian mother goddess, I felt like a combination of a dairy-cow and a cash machine. Stripped from any sense of a maternal identity, I felt like a "father" but one strapped to a breast pump and burdened by the weight of maternal guilt. Instead of embracing the feminist act of breadwinning, I felt reluctant, and sometimes embarrassed by it. I wondered if fathers felt like failures when they didn't see their children because they were breadwinning?

What is funny is that not only was I not poised to be the Stay-at-Home Mother my mother was, but my own mother had a Second Act as well. When I started college, she began adjuncting as a Hindi professor and soon became a full-time professor, attending conferences, and beloved by her students.

One of the things that was so hard about being a breadwinner for me was that growing up in a patriarchy, regardless of my media literacy, deep engagement with feminism, even decades of community organizing, I realized that I still aspired to be rescued. If someone admitted that to me, I would hurl a bell hooks book at them and tell them the story of when I saved my sister in a Wonder Woman bathing suit. But when I am being honest, I admit that this reluctance to be a breadwinner is deeply ingrained in me. I know that I am brainwashed by society's standards, and yet, I cannot help my desires. At the same time, acknowledging and being privy to my own brainwashing disgusts me, and therefore rouses me to fight it as I raise a daughter.

Now that my little girl is four, I want to embrace being a breadwinner and chuck out the reluctance forever. It helps that my husband has finished his teaching certification requirements, is almost done with his masters, and has started teaching. We still hold on to the future vision that our financial responsibilities will be shared, especially as he establishes himself in this new career. He is ambitious, and I continue to believe in him. And he has given me the opportunity to earn not only for the family but also for my own creative career – one that doesn't provide much in the way of money but gives me the outlet I need.

Seeing things from this perspective reminds me that the "rescue" fantasy is really terrifying in a lot of ways. Asking a man, even one I love and have children with, for money for a new bra (as a friend recently had to do) is more than I could bear. I embrace my freedom, and I am trying to embrace being the woman, and mother, that I am becoming.

Looking back, when I see pictures of me in that bathing suit, I admire how un-self-conscious I looked and felt. How fearless and free. For me, that was the gift of being a child. And perhaps that feeling of fearless freedom can be the gift that I give to my own daughter – a feeling she can hold on to throughout her life.

Modern Mythologies

Surya Kundu

Once upon a time, the story began, Prince Rama's scheming stepmother arranged to have Rama thrown out of his kingdom and exiled to a forest for fourteen long years. And so he went, and with him went his loyal brother Lakshman and his devoted wife Sita.

Like princes in exile, our parents too left their homes. There were no whispers from the lips of schemers, only the siren calls of opportunity. Some came for a chance to make money, others for adventure, most hoped to return to the country and families left behind. They traded familiar, if not palatial, grounds and set forth for the foreign forests and valleys of America.

The princes and Sita traded in their royal lives for those of forest dwelling ascetics. Leaving fineries behind at the palace gates, they continued in simple garb and simple ways.

Bristly carpets replaced cool stone floors, the comfort of sarees traded in for the utility of denim jeans. The warmth and the light of Calcutta were gone; jackets were purchased for the cool and foggy climes of Northern California.

As the days went by, life in the forest continued. Wandering through jungle trails, Rama and Lakshman met and defeated many Rakshasas, the fierce demons of mythology. While the men performed acts of heroism, the ever-dutiful Sita watched and waited.

My father went to work every morning, proving his worth to those who could not pronounce his name. My mother learned to shop in sterile and fluorescent grocery stores, miles away from the loud communal outdoor markets of her youth. Cocooned inside our tiny apartment and away from the grandparents I loved, my three-year-old self counted days till the end of our exile and our return.

One day, much like any other, Sita spotted a golden deer. Entranced by its beauty, Sita was consumed by the desire to possess the deer. "I must have it!" she cried, begging her husband and brother-in-law to fetch it for her.

Return tickets were purchased, trips were made, but still the golden promise of American employment lingered. One-way fares became round-trip, one apartment gave way to the next, and each time we returned. A few more months, we said, a few more years, just a little bit more time until we are home for good. One more chance to catch our fortune, we reasoned, wherever it may take us.

Rama and Lakshman prepared to set forth, but not before considering the protection of Sita, the innocent and helpless woman. Around their hut a circle was drawn. As long as she remained within its bounds, Sita would be protected from any evil that may come upon her.

Our parents too drew protective circles around us, carefully piecing together spheres of Indian culture in which they could raise their daughters. I grew up speaking English at school, but Bengali was the only language allowed at home. After homework was done, I learned how to read and to write in the same script as my cousin back in Calcutta. Monday afternoons were for dance lessons, classical Indian of course, and Saturday mornings were for voice lessons. Instead of Sunday morning cartoons I had Sunday morning Hindu school. What I lacked in early 90s pop culture, I made up for in Bengali poetry recitation and acting roles in the expat theater productions. Meticulous as they were, my parents still couldn't keep American culture out forever.

As Sita waited for Rama and Lakshman to return she heard the calls of a holy man outside her hut. Custom required that she invite him in and serve him, after all one must show respect. Sita hesitated, she knew that if she left the circle she risked being exposed to danger. If she didn't leave the circle to invite the man in, she risked flouting tradition. Thinking that generations before her couldn't have been wrong in their customs, Sita decided to invite him in. As soon as she left the ring to extend that invitation the holy man showed his true form – Ravana, king of the Rakshasas, who had come to take her away.

My parents had turned our home into the country they remembered, but every morning they were forced to turn me over to the world outside. The second I set foot on school grounds their protective charms dissipated and America took hold. Education is highly valued of course; the key to being respected in Indian American society is to be educated. Not only did my parents have to educate me, they had to encourage me to excel in this education.

So, to follow tradition, my parents let school in. Spoken Bengali ceded to the many shelves overflowing with English books. For the sake of education, I studied American history and English literature alongside the biology and calculus that were more recognizable to my parents as necessary curriculum. The debate team took me even further outside my parents' worlds as I traveled the state each weekend all in the name of being a better candidate for college.

To my parents' shock and surprise, the revered education began to morph into a strange being that was stealing their daughter away. School wasn't the only infiltrator, it brought along new ideas and options none of us had even dreamed of considering. The more I learned, the more I left the bubble around me. My goals were changing and one day my feet followed my sights to distant horizons.

Like other parents, mine had hoped that their circles would keep me close to home during college. Instead, I picked one on the opposite side of the country. Away from the Bay Area, my intellect headed down roads I hadn't even known existed. I strayed off the well-worn paths of science and math and gravitated towards the liberal arts and humanities. New ideas filled my mind. Once I had dreams of being a doctor, now I spent my days discussing feminism and systemic inequalities. I spent months in foreign countries, took weekend trips, and relished every opportunity to break a new boundary.

My parents, I imagine, must have been confused. I had once been their perfect child, mastering every facet of Bengali culture they had presented to me. I had thrived within their carefully constructed world, but suddenly I was outside of it living a life they had never foreseen. I was, quite literally, foreign to them. Of course they didn't approve of my choices: these choices only led me further away from them. At first, I tried to repair the distance.

After many long years and many fierce battles, Rama and Lakshman reached the distant shores where Sita had been taken. Reunited with her family at long last, Sita was overjoyed and ready to return with them back to the city they had left so long ago. Rama and Lakshman hesitated. Sita had spent such a long time away, among foreigners, how could they accept her back? They needed to be sure that she hadn't lost her honor and her virtue so they demanded that she prove herself by taking the agnipariksha – the fire exam. Rama needed proof that she had been faithful to him and nothing – no tears, no promises, no words – would do except a walk through fire. She walked unscathed, but that wasn't enough.

Every time I returned to California and to that world, I faced new scrutiny. Peers I had known for years wondered if my time at my New England college with its elite reputation had "white-washed" me. Others wondered at my academic choices; had I lost focus in my life? Of course not, I answered. I was actually taking classes on Indian history and Indian culture. To prove my strong ties with my heritage I was even planning on spending the summer in India working with slum children! I was proud as I made that announcement, certain that despite my non-traditional academic choices I was proving my worth as an Indian-American girl. What could be better proof than spending my time working to uplift the motherland herself?

Instead of the approval I'd anticipated, I heard a resounding chorus of "but you will be going alone??"

Confused, I asked why that mattered.

"India," they replied, "is not like America, it is not safe the way you are used to and you are not used to the customs."

"But Aunty," I countered, "America is not that safe either. More people carry guns here than in India, and I've already travelled alone to many places I wasn't used to! Plus, I'm probably going to spend two years after college teaching in some of the roughest neighborhoods in the country!"

All my facts were waved aside with one simple statement.

"But this is different; you are a girl."

Suddenly, the game had changed. My parents and their friends had pushed India and Indian culture upon me my entire life, but when I was making an independent choice to revisit that world, it was somehow a mistake. I didn't understand why, but my gender apparently justified standards and expectations that shifted and twisted and were seemingly impossible to live up to.

In the years that have passed since this announcement, I have tried over and over again to understand that reaction and its implication. I've tried to rationalize and see things from the perspective of the older generation, but every attempt leaves me just as confused. I knew, though, that while I may have made the "wrong" decisions, there were plenty of other girls who were still "good." As any good anthropology major would, I did some sleuthing to figure out what was going on.

I relied on sophisticated research methods – I opened up Facebook and looked up the girls I had known for years. Certainly no one could accuse them of being "white-washed" – most of these women were a part of South Asian organizations and had primarily South Asian friends. Boyfriends, if any, were also Indian and majors tended to be on the spectrum of math, science, and engineering. As I probed further, though, the pictures changed. The same groups of women would be at Bhangra club practices in one photo and Vegas clubs the next. Outfits switched from salwars to jeans to booty shorts. Almost every single person I looked up was leading two lives – one that their families saw and another that was only one password-protected page away.

That's when I realized the difference between these girls and me. To be "good" meant to live within that circle of cultural norms and community protection, or at least appear to do so. Of course, the others had their secret lives, but their parents didn't have to confront that truth daily or openly. I never lied about who I was and so neither could my family. My dissent and my independence were on display to the world – the traits that made up the bold print of my professional resume were the same ones that put me on the bad side of "good."

I tried, over and over again, to reconcile honesty and this rigid idea of goodness. Instead of retreating or turning my back on them as dinosaurs from the past generation, I attempted to share my new world with my parents. I made my choices – to attend a non-traditional (for most Desi kids, at least) college, to study a non-traditional subject, to pursue a non-traditional career in teaching, but at each step I was transparent about my reasons and tried to reassure them and get them on board. Even when I succeeded in convincing them, they still didn't openly discuss my life with their own families. After much explaining, they at least approved of me in private but still asked me to modify who I was in front of others. So much hiding and half-truth, all for the sake of a set of stereotypes and standards I didn't agree with.

Sita could not rest after one trial by fire. After the triumphant return from exile Prince Rama was poised to take his position as king. All around, the ministers and courtiers buzzed with rumors of Sita's years in the foreign Lanka. Sensing the brewing scandal, Rama asked her to repeat the agnipariksha, this time in the presence of all. Again, after enduring exile, abduction, and captivity, she was still being scrutinized. This time not just for her husband, but for her husband's advisors to see and judge. No one was concerned about her state or feelings, just with her chastity. A frustrated Sita chose to leave instead of submit again. Years later, hunting in the same forest he once lived in, Rama came across two children of superior physical talent. He followed them to their mother – none other than his own estranged wife. Rama wanted to bring them back with him to the palace but only if Sita took the test. Asked again to swallow her dignity and pride, Sita instead appealed to the earth and chose to be swallowed up into the land itself ending her story and her trials.

I'd been walking the walks of metaphorical fire for a while, trying to prove at each step that I was making the right choices, that I could be successful on my own and in my own ways. Walking those walks was exhausting. I was caught between conflicting ideas, the same ideas I'd been taught as a child. I'd been told to be honest, but being honest about my desires just created conflict with my family. I'd been told to have ambition and pursue knowledge, but that pursuit was landing me in trouble. I was struggling, but admitting that meant admitting defeat. Like Sita's, my walks were ultimately futile – very real virtues were overlooked for some fictitious idea of goodness. I understood Sita though, better than I ever had in all my years of Sunday Hindu school. Unlike Sita, however, I had (and still have) no intentions of being swallowed up by anything. I had to find new role models. Luckily, I didn't have to look far. My family, besides being Indian, is Bengali. Aside from an absurd fondness for fish and sweets, Bengalis also have a strong tradition of Goddess worship, especially Durga and Kali. These two women are the heavyweight female contenders of the Hindu Pantheon. Their arms (literal and metaphorical) rival those of contemporary superpowers. Both were called to aid the Gods in battle situations. Twice, powerful demons reigned supreme, immune from death if inflicted by a man. These demon kings never expected a woman to dare fight or even be capable of it. Far from being meek, both these women flaunt their power over arrogant demons and men.

Durga carries her trademark trident with her and Kali forgoes jewelry, choosing instead a necklace made of the skulls of her enemies. The two women differ in appearance – Durga, the composed and elegant warrior, and Kali, a vision of raw energy and power. Fearsome and magnificent, they are loved and revered by hundreds. Every year the largest festivals in Calcutta are those that honor these two women. No celebration is more raucous than the ten days of Durga Puja. Drums are played and lights are strung on every street as people young and old revel in new clothes bought especially for the occasion. Kali Puja brings with it loud fireworks and feasting. All this outpouring of devotion not for the men, but for the two Goddesses who put the Devi in deviant.

Our mythology tells us two things: Women who are unnecessarily asked to prove their worth prefer death by chasm, and women who break norms and dare do what men can't are the saviors of humankind. Forced submission kills while the daring are celebrated. As we celebrate our Goddesses though, Indian daughters everywhere are asked to be Sita. They are told to respect and revere strength but expected to fear the unfamiliar. We pray one way but practice another.

So I had a new story to mold my life around. I went to India – not just once, but twice during college. While there, I met other Devis – brilliant young women who had taken up arms against the demons of poverty, femicide, and illiteracy in their communities. As I helped them with their battles, I started the process of ending mine.

But my battles weren't against my parents, but against the misconceptions we held of each other. My parents saw me as rejecting their culture and heritage. At that point, I was so frustrated and angry that I had stopped seeing them as rational human beings. Neither perspective was true, and we needed many honest and occasionally painful conversations to realize that.

My parents, and many like them, fear that if a daughter is too independent, then she has been lost. The same stereotypes that fence us in also bind us to them, keep us from flying away to even more distant lands. My independence, though, is not an act of rejecting my culture, my heritage, or my family; instead, it's an act of reclaiming the traditions of feminism and power that have somehow gotten lost.

I don't follow stereotypes, I don't stay in circles, nor do I walk through fire. I choose my own definitions. I choose what being Indian means to me. I choose not to watch Bollywood, but I do choose to listen to classical music and to study Indian voices and to write about them too. I choose to share my culture and my own definition of it. I choose to cultivate my intellect, no matter where in the world that takes me. I choose my friends by the quality of their personalities, not by where their families came from. I choose to be a feminist, to be positive about my gender and my abilities. I choose to be honest about my life and what I do and with whom. I choose to be independent and strong, and I choose to be my own Goddess who I can worship and respect and love. Most of all, I choose my culture, not out of obligation or fear, but as it can be redefined by me.

Without Shame

Ayesha Mattu

Your task is not to seek for love, but merely to seek and find all the barriers within yourself that you have built against it.

~ Mevlana Jalāl ad-Dīn Muhammad Rūmī

In the Saratoga, California, private school I began attending in third grade in the early 1980s, intelligence, wealth, and crushes were important.

Abu was a cardiologist, Dadaji a principal, and further generations back on both sides of my family were farmers in the Punjab of an undivided India. But my new, mostly white, classmates? Most could count multiple generations of wealth and privilege.

As the new girl learning her place, I watched the eight-year-old couples proclaim they were "going around" with each other, which meant chaste hand-holding for a few minutes at recess before going their separate ways (girls to the play structures, boys to the field). After the bell rang, I returned to the serious work of bringing home the straight A's that my parents expected.

I was the only brown girl in my grade. Coming from a majority white public school, my new private school was similarly non-diverse. What was different was the presence of a little brown boy of Indian heritage in my grade: Raja.

These were the rules: In the Christie Brinkley era of beauty, perfection meant blonde hair and blue eyes. If you were a girl of East Asian heritage you could still be desirable, *if* you were smart, athletic, and chosen by one of the white boys. But if you were a brown girl? Not a chance. The only person ranked lower on the desirability scale than me was the sole black boy in our entire school, who happened to be in my grade.

In another time and place, Raja and I might have been separated by a militarized border. But here, in this country that persisted in perceiving itself as young and history-less, he and I were the same, in the eyes of others and myself. With elementary school love in the air and limited choices, I decided that he must be my soulmate.

My three-ring binder with the wide-eyed orange kittens on the cover sat on my desk. I opened the green Mead notebook held in place inside to a fresh page and scrawled the fateful, crooked cursive words with my gnawed-upon, bright yellow pencil: *I love Raja.*

I knew something was wrong when I saw Abu follow Ami into my bedroom. Given his busy schedule at the hospital clinic and nights on call, he was rarely at home to greet my two younger sisters and me in the morning or tuck us in at night.

I drew up my legs under the blanket, seeking to make myself as small and inaccessible as possible. My mother held my binder in her lap, her beautiful full lips pursed in the same way my grandmother's did when upset.

"Beta," she began, in a hesitant voice. "We found something in your notebook."

With the constant commentary at home and in our immigrant Pakistani community about "those Americans" and their different ways, I knew that I had done something wrong. But I didn't know why until Abu explained.

"You're a good Pakistani girl. A Muslim girl. We don't believe in this love-shove business," my father interjected.

He had witnessed the birth of a pure, new nation, one fought for by his parents, and wrested from the grasp of British colonists and Indians alike. No daughter of his was going to besmirch that with even the most innocent of crushes, especially not on a Hindu boy.

I knew then that I could never come to them. Never tell them what was in my heart, or the longings further down still. I wasn't allowed, meant, or created to love or desire.

A silence descended upon me, cloaking my heart and loins in an expanse as smooth and decorous as that between my Barbie's legs.

Years later, as I approached adolescence, Ami stirred the silence between us.

"My mother didn't prepare me, jan. I was fourteen and thought I was dying," she said by way of explanation, handing me a discreet brown paper bag with bulky sanitary pads inside.

Her hands were already beginning to bend under the bone-deep aches that would trouble her for years to come, but she touched my hair gently, like a blessing.

"Remember, boys only want one thing," she continued, color rising.

After handing down the foreknowledge of menstruation and sex that she had lacked, she retreated into silence again, having bettered the generations that went before her.

I looked into the mirror, wondering what it was that she saw in me. Someone desirable (though incapable of desire)? Yet, desirable only because of that which I held between my legs, not because of who I was as a person.

As the "darkest" sister of three, my family made it clear that my marriage would not be for my achievements, beauty, or personality, but as a complement to the "reputation" of my family – which really meant my father, his position and wealth.

Every day at school my classmates made it clear too, as they drew off into increasingly intense couplings while I remained unchosen, invisible, inviolable.

Working in the human rights sector in Islamabad after college in Massachusetts would liberate me from the duality of the immigrant child's existence in the US, the constant and exhausting *"But where are you really from?"* asked by white people who couldn't fathom a brown person truly belonging here, no matter what our blue passports said.

In Pakistan, I also discovered that I was not, as Abu had insisted, "only Pakistani." My hyphenated existence needn't be a fault line running through my soul, or a side to be chosen. I was teeming with multitudes, histories, and deep roots. I was blessed, complete. I claimed both countries for myself and swallowed them whole.

The non-profit I worked for had a small staff with a start-up fervor to eradicate child sexual abuse in a country that had no language for that abuse, in which few children were ever taught any names for their private body parts, and in which sexuality was rarely discussed or acknowledged.

Working to amplify the stories of children who had been sexually abused finally loosened my own shamed tongue. I applied for grants from European non-governmental organizations; gave presentations to journalists, parents, ambassadors, and teachers; and proudly told my mother's friends in formal drawing rooms that I was working to address jinsi tashadud – a term our executive director had coined to translate "sexual abuse" into Urdu.

Simply speaking those words silenced entire roomsful of aunties. I could see them balancing in their minds the commendable act of helping children with the utter shame of the body.

Ami never reprimanded me during my unseemly outbursts, though she often blushed. She simply served chai in English porcelain teacups to the stricken aunties, and, afterward, signed checks to support my organization.

ॐ

There is power in words. No wonder Ami and Abu had been afraid, kept me safe in an extended childhood, perhaps hoping that without the words (and with firm boundaries) I would never experience the dangers of desire or love or longing.

How wrong they were. How I wished I could have taken refuge in them each time I loved and lost. Instead, I had only the flat façade of the good Muslim girl, someone whose heart would switch magically on only after I settled down with my husband.

Long past my "sell by" date of twenty-five years of age, when all my loved ones had given me up to a life of spinsterhood, I met him, the man who would become my partner.

After their initial shock, my parents welcomed this white American man too. It was only the second love marriage in my extended family, and the first to a non-Pakistani. Perhaps it was the fact that my younger sisters were safely married or spoken for, perhaps it was because I was on the threshold of thirty, or perhaps, in their desperation, anyone with a pulse would have done.

I like to think that it was also because they realized that he saw me for who I was and loved me in a way they'd told me all my life I could never be loved or desired. And they saw that I loved him in exactly the same way.

They wanted me to be happy.

ॐ

It wasn't until after my marriage that Ami began talking to me about love, sex, and relationships in excruciating detail. Now that I was safely married, the fear and worry that had stoppered her mouth vanished, and decades of stories shot high as a geyser out of her.

Sometimes, I squirmed in embarrassment and wanted her to stop, especially when it came to her relationship with my father. But I also loved many of the stories she'd heard in the Pakistani village of her youth: the beautiful young woman who dressed up as a man and eloped one night with her lover; the girl who became pregnant outside of wedlock and was married off to an elderly man; the Sufi stories in which consummation was followed by the death of the lovers, for how could such a pure love survive in this world?

It was as a married woman that I found the more communicative mother I had wished for my entire life.

※

I grew up with women: my ever-present mother, two younger sisters, a tight-knit gang of high school friends, and four badass older cousins who spoke fluent Punjabi and could wield a delicate yet deadly Kolhapuri chappal at any man giving them the eye.

A girl. I'd always wanted a daughter. I'd take her by the hand and teach her to love her sacred body and her skin no matter what her complexion. I'd tell her she deserved to be seen and loved for everything that she was and longed to be.

My son arrived on a winter day in San Francisco in 2010. I held him in my arms, so recently released from the water inside me, this unknown being I had no idea how to mother or raise into manhood.

I would start, I vowed, by teaching him all the names.

※

It was my time in Pakistan that infected me with an immigrant's longings, that helped me understand my parents better. I returned to the US after working there in the human rights sector, having morphed in the process from second-generation to Generation 1.5, always half-glancing at the people and land left behind, always seeking to carry those seeds forward and plant them in this rich new soil of country and infant son.

The day my son stopped speaking his mother tongue, Urdu, at the age of two and switched over to English, I understood the anguish Ami had felt when I began kindergarten and refused to speak Urdu, and all the rejection that that must have implied.

But, I also realized that everything I give my son is a gift, for him to decide what to do with. Mothering is constant love, constant letting go.

ஃ

Foreplay is sunnah; orgasm a Muslim wife's right. (Funny how the men who shout loudest about their own rights forget their most basic responsibilities.)

When my husband and I had a child, we decided that we would share with him the frank, sex-positive Islam that has existed throughout history. That included not saying "down there" as many of our American friends were doing, but using the correct terms for all his body parts.

Having worked on abuse issues, I knew that giving children knowledge about their bodies, the permission to say "no" to adults when it came to physical interactions (even if relatives took offense), and an open line of communication with their parents was critically important to their health, bodily autonomy, and well-being.

My parents were not comfortable with all of our decisions but went along with them. They refrained from saying "shame-shame" when my toddler went through his long streaking phase. They sat with rigid smiles on their face and eyes seeking escape when he asked questions about *their* private parts. They endured when he chortled his new discovery that, "Mama has a vagina! Womens have vaginas!"

Generally, they showered him with love despite their discomfort and our departure from what they considered proper parenting.

I was out one afternoon, having left my son at my mother's house. She was hosting a formal tea with multiple trolley carts laden with delicious, meat-stuffed fried foods and ghee-rich desserts for a pair of newlyweds.

The couple shared their wedding album and spoke of their future plans. My two-and-a-half-year old son played nearby.

"Nano," he piped up in that shriek toddlers consider an indoor speaking voice. "This is my penis!"

He pointed proudly to his diapered crotch area.

"Hein?" my mother replied, choking on her tea, playing up her deafness in an attempt to deflect him, looking around desperately for someone to take him away.

My ten-year-old niece grinned on a nearby sofa, eager for the show, ignoring my mother's pleading eyes.

My sociable son toddled from person to person in the drawing room, introducing himself and then asking with great curiosity, "Do *you* have a penis? I have one – right here!"

The bride, a nurse, blushed and spluttered in Urdu, "What type of things have you taught him? I would never teach my child such filth!"

Eventually, my sister, who had three curious children of her own, came in from the kitchen, stifling her laughter. She led my son from the drawing room to distract him with toys and books.

As they left the room, he gleefully began singing a song at the top of his lungs, the words of which went something like this: "Penis, penis, peeeeeeeeeenis!"

My long-suffering parents were humiliated. The bride never contacted us again.

৯৹

When I heard what had happened, I laughed until I wheezed, tears streaming down my reddened face, hugging my badmash bachcha close and covering him with kisses.

But, I also sympathized with how excruciating it must have been for my restrained mother in particular. I realized that my parents had been right in one aspect at least, that there is a place and a time to talk about body parts and bodily functions, and that time usually isn't over high tea with one's aging grandparents and their guests.

My husband and I still laugh about our five-year-old's boisterous penis songs, his absolute adoration of his own marvelous body, and how he knows exactly which people will be most mortified by his chants and questions.

Though for years there was only rage, I see now that my parents tried their best. They tried to lessen the pain that they had inherited and which they, in turn, passed on to us. Ami, in particular, tried her best. Increasingly I feel the threads of generations unspooling into infinity both behind and in front of me, and I realize that with each successive generation we're lucky if we inch forward, if we manage to do less harm, if we can convince our children through our actions of our abiding love.

After the high tea drama and with kindergarten on the horizon, I started gently emphasizing the appropriateness of certain words and concepts in public versus private settings, but always with the understanding that his body is sacred, beautiful, worthy of protection – as is everyone's around him. That there are no words or stories, desires or questions, he cannot articulate to us.

I will continue to teach him that love and kindness are his rich Islamic, Pakistani, and American heritages and birthright. And I hope to continue showing him that he can always come to us, about anything – without shame.

The Day I Found Out I Was a Witch

Fawzia Mirza

"You have to change," my mother said.

"I am not going to change," I answered.

I was looking directly into her eyes – for the first time in my life without flinching and, even though I was terrified, without fear.

"You are possessed. You are possessed by the devil. The devil is in you," she said.

When I shared what had happened with my friend Alia, she said, "Your mother is scared. She's scared because you've never been so sure of yourself. You've never been so strong. You've never been so unapologetically you. You're coming into your power. You're a witch." I was laying on my younger brother's bed, my body and head under the covers. It was the eve of Eid-ul-Adha, the Feast of the Sacrifice, the celebration that marks the end of the yearly pilgrimage to Mecca to perform the Hajj – one of the holiest of holidays in the Muslim calendar.

"A witch?" I asked. I was silent and still. Only my eyes widened as I absorbed Alia's words. No one had ever called me a witch before. I didn't know how to react.

I'd never thought about being a witch before. In fact, I didn't think about witches much at all. I definitely didn't think about witches as something good or something to aspire towards. I associated witches with Salem and fire and men hating on women.

A witch, according to Merriam-Webster's Dictionary, is one who is "credited with usually malignant supernatural powers" or "a woman practicing black witchcraft often with the devil." Other definitions call a witch a sorceress, a woman who has evil or wicked magical powers, one who practices Wicca, an old hag.

I don't think my mom thought about witches either. She definitely didn't raise me to be a witch. She raised me to be a good Pakistani woman.

Being a good Pakistani woman meant also knowing how to be a good Pakistani wife, which meant knowing how to be a domestic superhero: separate the whites from the darks, iron men's shirts, wash cilantro three times before using it. I knew how to cook and clean, I came from a good family, I was educated, I could play the French horn, and I could speak Urdu and French. I was not a witch; I was a well-rounded brown girl ready to meet the brown man of my dreams.

My dreams and my mother's went something like this: I'd be introduced to a boy, a Pakistani man who was a doctor and the son of … a doctor. He and his parents would come to my house and sit in our drawing room. I'd make my dramatic entrance wearing a freshly starched, peach shalwaar kameez. I'd politely, properly, and ever so Pakistanishly, greet his parents, "As-salaam-alaikum," then him, my brown Prince Charming. I'd politely excuse myself to the kitchen, make a fresh pot of chai, and bring it in on a silver tray with a plate of hot samosas and chutney sandwiches. I'd serve everyone, including him. I'd hold the tray as he poured his tea. He'd smile at me; I'd smile back. And in that instant, we'd know: this was the beginning of our brown fairy tale. The End.

Clearly, I watched a lot of Bollywood movies. And Meg Ryan movies. And Disney movies. And the only witches in these stories were evil troublemakers who were unhappy in their own lives and therefore caused misfortune for others. No one ever wanted to be the witch.

Now, being a good Pakistani woman and wife also meant being a virgin; after all, virginity is the greatest Edible Arrangement you can give your husband. It comes right after "don't drink" and "don't dine on the swine." It's not like I was expected to have sex on my wedding night on a towel then show the bloody thing to my mother-in-law, but sexing out of wedlock was a big no-no.

So by the age of twelve, I wasn't allowed to hang out with boys, hug boys, or talk to boys on the phone, and I was not allowed to go to prom. This was devastating to twelve-year-old me because I desperately wanted to be like all the other girls: go to the mall, loiter over fingernail polish colors and milkshakes, hold hands at the movies, buy a really ugly fuchsia dress I'd only wear once, and slow dance to Celine Dion's "My Heart Will Go On."

Lucky for my mother and my virginity, back then boys weren't trying to jump down my shalwaar. My body didn't conform to the limiting standards of beauty that the white, male, hetero-normative gaze projects onto fashion magazines and television: I was a size 14 with long, jet black hair that fell down to my butt ... and also went across my cheeks, my forehead, my upper lip and, well, everywhere. I looked like a brown Ewok. My mother, whose idea of beauty was also pretty skewed, didn't ever call me overweight, she just called me "healthy" and "big boned." I wanted to attract my Prince Charming and for the boys to see me for the Princess I was on the inside. But no one could see the good Pakistani wife and woman that I was because they were too lost in the jungle of my eyebrows.

However, in this mess of hair and longing, I was allowed to hang out with girls. My best friends were girls. I made them laugh. I was a good listener. I shared my experiences and struggles, they felt safe and comfortable enough to share theirs with me. And my mother's advice kept ringing in my ears. "Be a good Pakistani woman, stay away from the boys." So I did.

I hit thirty and found myself going to gay bars. The girls I met listened to me and liked me for me, no matter what I was wearing. They were willing to talk about life and stayed engaged without staring at my chest or being distracted by Sports Center. They also were very beautiful and kind and strong and cool and fierce. And these girls had so much love to give. And so did I. And some of these girls went from being my girl friends to being my girlfriends, you know what I'm saying?

But how are you supposed to tell your mother that suddenly you date girls when you were never allowed to date at all? How are you even supposed to tell yourself? I was terrified of not making my dreams come true, or my mother's dreams for me come true.

I was living with a woman for three years who my mother thought was my roommate because, well, I told my mother she was my roommate. But when we broke up, I was incredibly sad and wanted to chat with someone who loved me unconditionally – I knew that one person was my mother. I was traveling the day sadness struck. I was on my computer and my mom appeared on Google Chat. We started chatting and I shared my sadness with her. It feels so easy sometimes, typing feelings and truths rather than saying them out loud. I didn't have to look my mother in the eyes when I told her, I just saw her little name in an Arial-like font. And so I blurted out that the girl I was living with was not my roommate. I told her she was my girlfriend. My mother didn't know what to say. We didn't speak for months afterwards except she'd send me verses from the Quran. I didn't respond. Then, I'd send her chat messages telling her I loved her and that I was the same daughter, but we did not speak.

The first time I saw her after that was when my brother had his son. We all flew to Baltimore to meet my nephew in the hospital. He was so wrinkly and brown and cute and innocent. I held him and cried. My mother hugged me and cried, but the whole time I was there I felt like I was the weird stranger who had barged in on some other family's happy moment. We kissed and hugged the new addition to our family, but we never talked about what I had told her.

One day, I came home for Eid. I came home only for the weekend. I didn't want to see anyone else in our Muslim community. I only wanted to share my time off with my mother. The conversation started with her disapproving looks and my questioning those looks.

"I don't approve. You have to change," she said.

"I am not going to change, Mom," I said.

"You have to change," she said.

"I am not going to change, Mom," I said.

"You have to change!"

"I am not going to change."

I was looking her directly in the eyes. Her eyes searched mine and I could see them bulge. And then I could see the fear in her.

"Something has happened to you," she said in Urdu. "You are possessed. You are possessed by the devil. The devil is in you."

And as tears came out of her eyes and mine, as we shared this moment of unprecedented emotional distance even though we sat only a foot away from each other, I said, "If you can't love me, I have to go. I have to go." I heard myself blubbering the words, like a three year old who's still formulating the English language.

"I have to go. I can't stay here." I stood and walked to my room and closed the door, my face wet. I jumped under the covers and cried. My entire body shook with the sadness I felt inside. I wanted to feel safe, to feel loved and understood, but in that moment I did not.

I called someone who could make me feel better. I called my dear friend Alia. She initially just listened and told me she loved me. And after I told her everything that happened, she said, "You're coming into your power. You're a witch." By this time my eyes were raw from crying but my tears had stopped. My chest hurt because I thought my heart was going to be pulled out of my body. Why did I think witches were scary?

Witches were thought to be possessed by the devil. By evil. But essentially they were just defiant and refused to remain silent and died for their identity.

My mother thought I was possessed by the devil. The devil symbolizes evil, bad, sin. I don't blame my mother for saying this: it's what was taught to her and is taught to many others.

But witches are powerful. Witches are magical. Witches have a strong community.

Witches have secrets. Witches are women who refuse to be controlled by others. Witches walk among us every day and say, "This is who I am, and I am proud of it." Witches are greatly misunderstood and therefore condemned.

So did that make me a good witch? No, I didn't need the qualifier. I'm coming into my power, I thought. I am powerful in being honest. I am powerful in sharing my truths. I am powerful in being me. Power scares people. Power scares my mother's idea of me. Power scares tradition. And that's when I knew. Her words suddenly gave me hope. I heard myself tell Alia, "You're right. I am. I am. I am a witch."

"The Only Dates Are the Ones You Eat"
and Other Laws of an Immigrant Girlhood

Nayomi Munaweera

I'm forty-one and at a gathering of Sri Lankans in Los Angeles. An (unrelated) uncle who I haven't seen decades says, "You're a writer now? Come and meet my friends. They want to know about your book." I am suspicious of older men in this, the diasporic community I grew up in, but writer's narcissism and the hope that they might actually want to know about my work overrides my skepticism.

He leads me into a circle of men and says, "This is Nayomi. She used to see ..." He names a sweetheart I haven't seen since I was twenty-four. An adolescent shame flares through my veins and I can only waggle my head in an ambiguous island gesture. The uncle says, "Can't even remember? So many boyfriends no?" The men cackle. All mention of my book is banished, instead I am pinned and defined. Species and genus uncovered: Bad girl/rebel girl/ slut. Judgments about female sexuality flood in and undermine everything else I have done with my life.

Gossip in our communities, both diasporic and at "home," is a system of control. A woman or girl's body is viewed as the property of the greater community. The way she dresses, who she talks to or dances with will be scrutinized, dissected, and sometimes used to assassinate her character. Whatever else a woman or girl may be, she will be first and foremost defined by her love life. If she has had a boyfriend or god forbid more than one (as I did), if she is divorced (as I am), if she doesn't choose to have children (ditto), she will be suspect and open to censure.

From the age of sixteen to twenty-four, growing up in Los Angeles, I had a boyfriend, worse yet, a Tamil boyfriend. Writing about this first relationship still feels like the uncovering of a shameful secret. In Sri Lanka, the Tamil Tigers and the Sinhalese military forces were fighting a civil war from 1982 to 2009, which would end up claiming an estimated 80,000-100,000 lives. I am Sinhala and when my community found out about my relationship with a boy from the "opposing side," there was hell to pay. At parties and family gatherings I was viewed with suspicion. The aunties warned their daughters away from me. They were afraid of a sort of sexual contamination by which their own virginal girls would be spoiled by talking to me or merely by being seen with me. My parents fell in line with these judgments to protect their own precarious belonging. As a young immigrant I was already alienated by the experience of landing in America and being one of the few brown kids in my school. This second othering, enacted by the immigrant community I was supposed to belong to, was profoundly painful.

Salman Rushdie once said, "Migration throws *everything* into crisis..." For me, nowhere was this truer than in the realm of sexuality and parental attempts to control it.

My family left Sri Lanka when I was three. We lived in Nigeria for nine years and then in 1984 we migrated to Los Angeles. Entering America at twelve, I was innocent in a way that would have been impossible if I had grown up here. I had never chosen my own clothes; I had never styled my hair. I had only worn school uniforms and regulation shoes. I did, however, know about sex. It was when a boy and girl sang loudly at each other and danced around trees. Sometimes it would rain and the girl's sari would cling to her wet skin, then shockingly they might press passionate lips on opposite ends of an apple. Bollywood was alive and well in Nigeria, and it formed all of my sexual understanding.

Now in America, I was thrust into a world where boys and girls casually held hands and tongue kissed (no apples!) against the lockers. I watched them, shocked by their brazenness and waiting for the adults who would come screaming to rip them apart. I knew they would not be called out at Morning Assembly and made to stand still while a teacher whipped at their legs with a slender whistling switch as would happen in Nigeria for much smaller infractions. But I expected there would be some punishment. It was startling to realize that there would be none. In this new world, there were boys who flirted and girls who wore luscious red lipstick. There was MTV and Madonna in ripped lace, there was Billy Idol with his sexy snarl and me in my ill-fitting, new (second-hand) clothes, desperately wanting to belong.

At home, my parents realized the powerful threat of contagion posed by Americanization, and wrapped my sister and me tight in an insulating cloak of Sinhala culture. On the weekends we went to the Buddhist temple, to cultural shows, and community parties. And like all the other Sri Lankan parents we knew, the most important rule of the house was the No Boyfriend Rule. "The only dates in this house will be the ones you eat," they said. It was a joke but it was also a law.

As part of their program of cultural conservation, my mother nagged me into being an usher at a Sri Lankan Variety Show when I was sixteen. She was hoping it would interest me in Sinhala music and Kandyan dancing. Instead, I met the bass player for the backup band. He was twenty. He was Tamil. He played bass! In a band! It didn't matter that it was a family band that played covers like "Hotel California" and "On Blueberry Hill." I had never met a Sri Lankan guy who made music, who didn't seem to care about the usual doctor/lawyer/engineer trajectory. This one wanted to be a pilot. More than all this, he actually liked me. We were together for the next eight years.

In Sri Lanka, the Sinhala make up a 70% majority and the Tamils make up a 13% minority. The war between these two ethnicities has also spread both peoples far into the international diaspora. We Sinhala were aware of the huge Tamil community in places like Lancaster, California, (which we called SriLankcaster), but mingling between our communities was rare because of the war. Yet what did this far-away war have to do with my boyfriend and me?

Everything.

This was a war funded by the diaspora. There were Tamils who sent money to the Tigers (either willfully or through coercion), there were Sinhala who sent money to the government. Vast quantities of money so that each side had more arms, tanks and bombs than they could ever have accessed without the weapon of diasporic longing. In London, Toronto, Melbourne, parts of the Tamil and Sinhala communities poured money into the coffers of these two fierce enemies, then sat back and let the boys and girls on the ground kill each other and themselves for 26 years. These enmities then carried back into our communities where Tamils and Sinhala people viewed each other with distrust and fear.

My boyfriend and I were unaware for the most part, of these greater forces. We had fallen in love. We had discovered something potent and delicious and dangerous. We kissed in his car; we met in the library and hid out in motel rooms. I lost my virginity a few miles away from my parents' house. I cried that afternoon. I knew I had lost something that could not be recovered, some child-self, some precious girlhood. But after that, sex was a powerful force. I had found something that belonged just to me, just to him. I had discovered pleasure. Sex was a way of saying, I choose America. Yet, I had also chosen a boy that bound me to struggles at home. The fact that we were loving each other, while in our shared homeland our two people were destroying each other held some special and deeper tenderness. Together, it felt like we were knitting together the broken; together it felt like we were becoming American.

At his home, they welcomed me. What did this mean from people who had fled the island in 1983 during anti-Tamil race riots? What did it mean to them that their son was dating a Sinhala girl when Sinhala mobs had almost killed them? They had been on holiday in Sri Lanka when the mobs had come; my boyfriend, his brother, and his sister had hid under the bed. There had been a terrifying midnight drive through looted, burning streets to the airport. They didn't talk about these memories often. But when they did, my ears were wide open. I was hearing a history hidden from most Sinhala people.

Of course, all of this was secret. At home my parents were still going on about edible dates. So I lied. A lot. I said I was candy striping; I left home in my uniform and then I changed at the library and met him in his car. The lies felt necessary for survival.

Our love affair was secret for a year and then an uncle, one who was very loudly anti-Tamil and pro the Sinhala government, called my parents and shouted that I was out of control, I was bringing shame upon the whole family. I had a boyfriend, he screamed. *A Tamil boyfriend.*

I have no idea how he found out. The grapevine must have been stronger than I had suspected. I came home and my parents were sitting stiffly on the couch. "Where were you?" they asked.

"At the library." I lied even as I saw how my words cut them. They screamed; I cried. I screamed; my mother cried. I said it was all worth it. They were shocked. I accused them of being racist, saying that they were mostly angry because my boyfriend was Tamil. My father shouted, "I went to university with Tamils. We are not racist." The unspoken caveat, "But we don't date them, don't sleep with them, don't love them."

They laid down the laws. I wouldn't see him anymore. They were taking away my car. My life would be confined to home, school, and studying. I felt as if my life was shutting down. I saw my freedom, a small feathered baby bird run over by the wheel of a car.

But I refused to give him up. Instead I kept lying and getting caught. My parents no longer trusted me. In our community the story spread fast and girls who had been my friends previously were not allowed to talk to me. Uncles said cruel and blatantly sexist, sexual things to me under their breath. *I was spoiled goods. I had thrown away my life and my reputation. My parents would never find a good Sinhala boy for me to marry. The stain would follow me for years.* We didn't have the term "slut-shaming" then, but this is exactly what it was.

This continued until I left for university. Later, at twenty-four, when I realized that I didn't want to marry this man, the fear of what the community would say kept me in that relationship for far too long. By this time, the pressure had changed direction. Now that I had been with him and had clearly been sleeping with him for so long, I had better marry the guy, was the community's dictate. But I broke that rule too, and then dealt with the next wave of gossip and ostracism that followed.

To this day, I am viewed, at least partially, as the girl who broke the No Boyfriend Law. Now, in retrospect, I wonder if my parents' reaction would have been as vociferous if they had not been confronted with my uncle's rage. Even worse than the boyfriend, *Tamil boyfriend,* was the fact that one of the pillars of the community had judged their daughter's behavior as shameful. They were worried that a relationship would disrupt my studies. But beyond this, they also needed to fit into the community, and having a daughter that *everyone* gossiped about was a huge liability. They longed for the approval of the Sinhala-Los Angeles community – it was the closest thing they had to the home they had lost. Meanwhile, I longed to belong to America.

I understand how hard migration was for my parents. They were brought up in a culture in which age was revered and youth was voiceless. My father obeyed his parents' every wish until he was in university. If he hadn't, there was an entire system to cut him down to size, aunties, uncles, even the village monk, *everyone* would get involved in guiding youth. *Everyone* was extended family; *everyone* had a say. So I can only imagine what a difficult transition it was for my parents to land in America and realize that here their daughters might openly defy them. My father describes it like this, "When small people become big, big people must become small." This description of them having to make themselves small to accommodate my rebellion hurts. I wish migration could have expanded their world as greatly as it did mine, yet, at least for those first painful years, it did not.

Another aspect of America they were unprepared for: new rules about female sexuality. Women's bodies were suddenly ubiquitous, displayed flagrantly, and used to sell every product imaginable. Where they came from, parents orchestrated marriages (including theirs) and when a groom and bride returned to his parents' house after their wedding-trip, they brought with them the blood-bloomed sheet proving her virtue. Without this proof of virginity, the new wife was worthless and might be abandoned without resources. Virginity could be a matter of life and death.

In choosing my first love, and consequently in choosing to have sex with him, I had broken ancient laws. My parents were astounded by my easy letting go of something that they had been trained to revere and protect. It led to a great deal of conflict, but I know that I got off easy. I've witnessed girls subject to so much worse, the uncle who punched his daughter for talking to a boy at a party, the aunty who forced her daughter into an arranged marriage with a much older man at the age of nineteen, the friend who broke mentally under the psychic pressure of having her every move being watched and talked about by *everyone*. The boxes they want to force us into are tiny. If you don't struggle to breathe, to gain your own voice, you can be suffocated. I've seen this happen over and over to young women in my community, and the results are tragic.

But what is far more important than what the community says about us is how we see ourselves. In 2007 when I first met the man who would become my husband, I explained that we couldn't tell anyone about our relationship. The fact that I was freshly out of a divorce and sleeping with this white man with no thought beyond the joy of it felt deeply shameful. We would have to keep it secret or *everyone* would talk about it I said. Mystified, he challenged me, "*Everyone*? Who is *everyone*? *Everyone* in the world?"

"No, of course not", I said, "Just … you know … *everyone*."

He said, "You mean the aunties and uncles in LA? You mean the tiniest fraction of a tiny diasporic community from a tiny island?" He said this and I saw the lie dissolve. I had internalized the community's gaze so deeply that it felt like *everyone* in the world was watching me with disapproving eyes. I had labeled *myself* "slut." I had brought the village my father grew up in to America. I had done this unconsciously, but so thoroughly, that despite my early rebellions, my decisions involving sexuality and love felt profoundly shameful if they did not conform to the community's dictates.

This push to silence, instilled in childhood and reinforced in adolescence, is alive well into adulthood. I remember once my mother and I were sitting at the kitchen table while my first husband (Sri Lankan) was upstairs. Offhand she said something disparaging about "the gays." Heart thudding, I said, "Don't say things like that. You know I'm bi-sexual right?" She looked panicked, "Shhh… don't talk about it. Your husband will hear." I said, "Ammie, he knows. It's okay. It's not a secret." But she shushed me again because she could hear my husband coming down the stairs. She warned me with her eyes to stay silent. An important part of me was shut away from her then, and, like many other things, we never talked of it again.

Even now, at the age of forty-one, it can be hard to claim my own narrative. Yet I am learning over and over that how the community views you, how anyone views you from outside the sanctity of your own skin, is a sad substitute for the power that can be gained from inhabiting your own story and your own sexuality. The scariest thing is to say, "I know you don't approve and that hurts, but I am privileged enough to live in a time and place where I get to decide who to love, how to love, who to fuck, how to fuck, and I will exercise these freedoms." To say this with compassion, both for their journey, as well as for my own, is the greatest challenge.

A few years ago, I was at a meditation retreat and saw the uncle who had ratted out my first relationship. We had all taken a vow of silence for ten days and every time I walked past him to my cushion in the front of the hall he craned his neck to stare. Was it the girl who decades before he had put in a little box with the tag, "Girl with boyfriend, *Tamil boyfriend*, girl with loose moral character?" Now he had to add, "meditator" to his list. Did this disrupt his classification? Was he forced to consider that a woman can be simultaneously rebellious *and* committed to spiritual practices deeply revered in our culture? I hope so. I hope he saw that I am much more than the sum of my sexual history.

Writing this essay has been difficult. Always, a voice asks, "What will people say? What are the repercussions to revealing vulnerability?" My stomach turns with the terror of revealing what I have been taught to keep secret. But greater than the fear is the hope that a girl like I was, a girl torn between two places, might find herself in my words.

If I could talk to her, and also to my own teenage self, this is what I would say: *You don't know it yet, but yours is the universal and bittersweet song of the immigrant. You may lose family, culture, a sense of belonging. It will be lonely, you will be adrift, the ones you love may not understand what you are becoming. You will lose the village of your father's birth, but you will gain your own pleasure and your own story.*

Patti Smith in the Dark

Jyothi Natarajan

My phone chirruped mid-morning with a message from my older sister Vani: "Damn. Vitamix just arrived. It's heavy. I may need a cab, honestly." That afternoon, a three-foot long, rectangular box was delivered to my office on the sixth floor of a building in Manhattan's flower district. It, too, had the word "VITAMIX" printed on it.

To my colleagues who noticed the package in the office, the appliance must have seemed an extravagant purchase – the Vitamix 5200 retails for around $450. When I told an office mate that the blender was a gift from my mom, and that my sister had gotten one today too, she nearly fell over.

This wasn't our first gift from Mom, but it had to have been the most pricey. It also came at a funny time in our lives: both my sister and I were, for the first time, living with serious romantic partners. But more importantly, both of us had decided, against our mother's wishes, not to get married. What, then, was the meaning of this powerful, domestic gadget – one that was capable of blending an iPhone to dust and which arrived just as we were rejecting her vision of domesticity?

જ

The motor of a Vitamix is as powerful as that of a lawn mower. Its blades move at speeds up to 240 miles per hour. Our mom bought her own Vitamix last year. "I've been in this country for over 30 years now," she told me soon after she made the purchase, "and for nearly that long, I've been wanting a Vitamix. And then my blender broke."

Mom arrived in the U.S. from Bombay in 1976. Newly married, she followed our dad back to a small suburban town in southeastern Virginia, where he had started an engineering job. I imagine her then, a twenty-five-year-old woman who was accustomed to jumping on and off buses in India's biggest, busiest city. She was now stuck in an apartment in a mostly white town in the American South and could only go anywhere when her husband drove her. I like to think her days were structured around cracking the code to this strange place where she had landed, driven along by unexpected moments of comprehension. She likes to tell us about how she'd listen to the radio on the highest volume to drown out the silence of small-town Virginia. The songs of the mid-to-late '70s that she memorized became an entrée to the American cultural spaces of school and work.

By the time my sister Vani was born in 1979, our mom, who had a bachelor's in chemistry from a university in Bombay, had begun an associate degree in computer science at a local community college. Three and a half years later, I would come along, and a year after that, Mom would start working full time, writing software for satellites launched on NASA rockets.

When I was in elementary school, I remember her sitting late at night at the dining table reading under a bright lamp. After coming home from work and cooking dinner, she would teach herself new computer languages. I could imagine how she wrestled with Java or C++ in the same way she wrestled with American English idioms in front of our teachers at school or her colleagues at work. Learning and knowing these languages was a way of moving forward and becoming able to act in the world. And so as a parent, it's not surprising that she would want to figure out her daughters, too – and how to act in our worlds. We were products not only of her household, but also of the small, white town she had settled in. She couldn't know of the micro-aggressions we experienced as young brown girls in suburban America or how the social values of our classmates and the discipline thrust upon us in the classroom gave us fuel to challenge her rules at home.

Mom likes to joke about how Vani and I were such rebels growing up. It's not that we were breaking many rules, but she saw much of our behavior and choices as incongruous with the unspoken rules of immigrant assimilation. We were unlike other young Indian American girls she had come to know. As a teen, Vani would spend hours in her room, with the lights off, staring at the ceiling and listening to Patti Smith. I would peek in from time to time, wondering what she had discovered in that darkness. I wanted to climb into that space, too. I'm not sure when, but at some point I started to see how my older sister's preoccupations – with music, art, books – allowed her to build a world that insulated her from our parents' discipline and from her school's quiet hostility.

By the time I was a teenager, my rebellion had taken shape largely through the artistic inheritance my sister accumulated. Mom and Dad liked to take us on periodic trips to Virginia Beach when we were kids to visit the nearest Hindu Temple, and we made it a point to stop on the way back at a large shopping mall outside the city that was home to Planet Music, an enormous warehouse-style record store. Inside were stations where you could sit, put on plush headphones, and listen to tracks from new albums.

On one of these trips, when I was in 6th grade and Vani in 10th, the four of us entered Planet Music and wandered off in opposite directions – Dad and Mom toward the extensive world music shelves that stocked albums by flutist Hariprasad Chaurasia and legendary qawwali singer Nusrat Fateh Ali Khan, and Vani over to the punk rock section. I shuffled along behind her. Until a few years earlier the only albums I had bought with my own money were MC Hammer's *Too Legit to Quit* and *The Three Tenors in Concert*. Vani had recently discovered the DC punk band Fugazi, and when I pleaded her to recommend an artist to me, she casually handed me the cassette tape for another DC-based band, Jawbox, whose new noise rock album *For Your Own Special Sweetheart* had just been released. "Try this one," she said.

I slipped the tape into my Walkman on the ride home and listened to it on loop for weeks. All our parents could hear from my headphones was the low-frequency thrumming of Kim Coletta's bass. "Chi! What is this noise? This music has no melody," Mom would complain. The dissonance of noise rock might have been illegible to our parents, but I reveled in its ability to create a space where I couldn't be understood by them, just as I imagined Vani had. In that illegibility I searched for a way into Vani's interior world.

I felt my role as little sister acutely. I sought out Vani's affirmation just as I sought out her tastes in music and books. But she was facing the other way, ready to set off into the world she had imagined into being through the novels that kept her up late at night. It wasn't until she left for college that she turned back around – for me.

৯৩

Sometimes the easiest or only way to express love and support within families is to keep secrets from each other, to withhold or avoid moments of vulnerability. As we were growing up, our mom treasured emotional intimacy, but sometimes the cocoon she spun felt too raw. I could tell Vani knew that early on. My sister's demonstrations of love were often accompanied with a well-timed joke. It's a skill, I knew, that she must have inherited from Dad, who was often punning his way through dinner. But Vani's puns did something more: they dissolved tension, deflected awkwardness, allowed us to laugh together. Her puns arrived just in time to steer Mom away from asking difficult questions she wasn't ready to answer.

But with me, Vani drew closer while she was away at college. She began to call me regularly, late at night. I'd sit on the couch finishing my homework and listen to her describe her latest encounter with a crush, how they brushed past each other in front of the library, or a testy late-night conversation with a friend across the hall. In those moments, tucking the receiver under my chin as the night wore on, I mostly listened, and in the pockets of silence I cobbled together a few reassuring words.

It was the summer of 2000, when Vani was working as a camp counselor at a high school creative writing camp and I was heading off to French Academy, a language intensive camp where I would spend three weeks speaking only French with a group of fifty other high school students from around Virginia. Vani had a week off between two sessions of camp, and she and my parents drove me out to Lynchburg, a city in the foothills of the Blue Ridge Mountains, to drop me off at the Virginia School for the Deaf and the Blind, which had been home to the language intensive for years.

It was an impossibly humid summer. Thick green foliage sweated beneath the hot sun. My parents settled me into a dorm room I'd be sharing with another girl and set up a large upright fan next to the window. In the final half hour we spent together before I would have to take an oath to swear off English for three weeks, Vani pulled me aside with a sudden tug. She whispered that she needed to tell me something. We walked outside and stood behind an enormous tree. She had met someone at camp. A woman. A fellow camp counselor. Vani drew me in close. "Jyothi," she started, "I am dating a woman. I wanted you to know. I'm gay."

I was about to say farewell to the English language for three weeks, and so I don't recall the exact words I shared with her. I remember giving her a tight hug, sharing a wide grin. I remember thinking, my sister's world has developed so many new layers since she left home. I can never know her fully. But she trusts me with this. The moment felt like learning a secret handshake with a best friend. One that we would practice and add to every time we met.

When Mom figured out for herself that Vani was dating a woman, she asked our dad to talk to Vani instead of speaking to her herself. The conversation, which has only been recounted to me by my sister, was uncomfortable. I can imagine Dad standing in our living room, clenching his jaw, afraid to hear the truth. When Vani spelled the situation out for him – that she was dating a woman whom she had met that summer – Vani remembers him asking her if she hated men, if she was influenced by the novels and books she had read as a teenager.

Our parents waded through molasses for the next six to seven years as they struggled to understand what Vani's life was becoming. Our dad almost never brought up the subject of her love life or her sexuality. Our mom broached it on tip-toe. Both thought they could coax Vani out of it. Our mom kept asking her why she wanted her life to be so difficult. It had been less than two years since Matthew Shepard was brutally murdered in Wyoming and the shadow of that incident gave shape to a fear our mom didn't realize she had. Would her daughter be accepted by society? Would she feel alone in the world? And would that lead her to close off from Mom?

When Vani didn't answer their phone calls as regularly, avoided situations where Mom and Dad could see her living space, and left out personal details of her life when she did talk to them, they started turning to me for reassurance. I had to find a way to make Vani legible to my parents. And in doing so, I had to make myself legible to them, too.

On trips home, as night closed in, I'd find Mom alone in her bed before Dad had finished watching his favorite late night TV shows. I'd stretch out next to her, both of us staring at the ceiling, her eyes puffy with tiredness and affection. She would begin asking a few questions about my life. And then move to Vani. We'd have long, meandering conversations punctuated by moments of silence when I'd realize she had nodded off. She'd ask a series of questions. What does "queer" mean? She'd ask whether Vani was happy being queer and I would tell her about my other LGBTQ friends, that many of them were perfectly happy. We kept meeting like this – always in her bed, always late at night – for years. She'd often ask the same questions over and over, as if with repetition these new ideas would sink in. But it wasn't always easy. The conversations continued over the phone in between those visits. Questions that I knew Vani could easily answer herself were being posed to me. I would get frustrated, filled with resentment. Why did I have to account for Vani's whereabouts, her happiness? How had I suddenly become the go-between, the mediator between my parents' fears and what they understood as my sister's rebellion?

In 2003, I started dating someone seriously, a college classmate named Anand. His father, a Maharashtrian Hindu man, had come to the U.S. just a few years before my dad had arrived for graduate school. His father, too, had studied engineering, and after taking a job at Purdue University, had fallen in love with a graduate student – a white American woman who had grown up Presbyterian in Indiana. They were married in 1975, in a ceremony that celebrated two cultural and religious traditions. Twenty years later, with three young children, they decided to move back to India, to Bangalore.

I bring up Anand's parents' story because although I didn't realize it when we started dating, he shared a set of cultural references not only with me but also with my parents – he arrived his first year in college as an international student, loved old Hindi film songs, followed Indian politics and even had a working knowledge of cricket. On top of that, he was compassionate, gregarious, and exhibited a social ease with Indian aunties and uncles. He knew just how to tilt his head, just how to fill out a friendly conversation.

We were adamant in telling ourselves that the reasons we fell in love had little to do with India. We were both involved in student organizing, had been active in anti-war demonstrations, and our leftist politics drove many of our choices as undergrads. We had a sense of ourselves as transgressive. We were both feminists – we rejected the terms "boyfriend" and "girlfriend" within our first weeks of dating.

As two Indian Americans in a relationship, we feared that we would fall easily into the expectations our parents had for us. We didn't want to be known only as "good Indian children."

But the cushion around us only grew. After our parents met each other, they started scheduling their own Skype dates without us around. My mom introduced Anand to her friends, and for her, the powerful approving gaze of the aunties amplified her comfort with our relationship. That gaze could so easily guide me into a role that was in fact uncomfortable to me. Being the mediator, the one who spoke regularly both to Vani and to my parents, meant being intelligible to both. But I was realizing that it was easy to slide from being on good terms with family to being seen as the "good" daughter—to Vani's bad daughter. And that realization was both illuminating and upsetting. As Anand and I elbowed up against the gaze, I felt the social pressure of our families descend on us. Were we going to join their team?

Several years later, after moving to New York City and beginning to work in publishing, I read a book by the novelist and essayist Sarah Schulman whose fiction about queer New York in the '80s Vani had introduced me to. The book, *Ties That Bind*, was a work of non-fiction about how homophobia takes shape within families. I carried the book around with me for weeks, read and reread pages describing scenarios of families shunning gay children, diminishing the importance of their lives with subtle gestures, turns of phrase. Many of the stories felt familiar – at family gatherings Vani and I attended together, relatives, some of whom Vani had come out to, showered me with attention and questions about my relationship with Anand, while they treated Vani with a distant caution. For many, especially those of our own generation, seeing someone like me gravitate toward a life like their own – complete with marriage, house, kids—kept their world intact. But that world, I worried, didn't have room for Vani.

At those gatherings, Vani and I would steal away to a corner of the room and roll our eyes at the affirmation I had just received. We were so used to this ritual. Conservative Indian family values, heightened in the diasporic context, had been reproduced all around us as kids. I searched for a way out. I wanted to build rooms for the two of us, in which Vani could take up as much space as I could. If I submitted to the approving gaze of aunts and uncles and cousins and followed through with the expectations of a good daughter, I'd be tearing myself away from my sister. I would be drawing a line between us that she could never cross.

That line, I knew, already existed. I was benefitting from privileges that I had no choice in upholding: the privileges extended to a straight daughter in a relationship with a fellow upper-caste (if multi-racial) Indian man. But choices still remained. In May of 2011, Anand and I decided that we wanted to have a party. A non-wedding party. We had just crossed the nine-year mark in our relationship, had traveled around the world to live with each other, and were figuring out a way to sustain a long-term, long-distance relationship. But we agreed that the life ahead for us didn't include marriage.

Neither of us believed politically in the institution of marriage. For some of our friends it was a path to regularize their immigration status, or to get access to the health care they needed. To us, it felt more like a way to appease family than a chance to honor and celebrate the love we shared. And if appeasing family led us down a path that excluded Vani, we wanted instead to turn around and follow her.

Our decision was met with confusion from our parents. They knew we had been skirting the subject of marriage, but to them it meant that we just weren't ready, or maybe that we were open to persuasion. "A non-wedding party? What is that?" my mom laughed over the phone. She thought of it as a farce. Ridiculous. Something I would grow out of. "What about all the legal benefits you would be forgoing?" she asked. Hospital visitation. Tax breaks. That, I told her, is precisely one of the reasons marriage as an institution is unfair. If an arbitrary rule exists that prevents you from visiting your lover when they're sick in the hospital unless the state has sanctioned your relationship, that rule seems bogus.

At that point, nearly every year Mom was attending a handful of weddings for children we grew up with in Virginia. She'd return from late night receptions stuffed from one too many gulab jamuns, dizzy from dancing to Bollywood remixes, and I could imagine herself asking why Anand and I didn't get married, too. These questions rose to the surface whenever Vani and I visited home. My sister would always come to my defense, coaxing Mom to understand. But it felt like our mom wasn't listening, or never had. How many times, I thought, did I have to explain this to her. Could she not wrap her head around me falling out of good daughter status? Our conversations took place as debates about marriage equality were raging across the U.S. More than a dozen states had lifted bans on gay marriage, and within a few years, the Supreme Court would rule five-four in favor of marriage equality.

Part of me wondered if Mom would ever ask Vani if she had plans to get married, now that it was legally permissible. Was this a battle that was just mine, as the straight daughter?

Vani met someone in the fall of 2012. He was a white trans man who had grown up in the Midwest and had made his way to New York for law school. As I grew to know Vani's partner over the next two years, I witnessed how the two of them brought out the most delightful parts of each other's personalities. He had been given a glimpse into my sister's interior world and had delighted in what he found. When Vani revealed to our mom that she was dating someone, the ground shifted. The fear that gripped our parents' first reaction to Vani coming out – that she would feel isolated and lonely in an intolerant world, that she was making her own life difficult – had loosened from its tight sockets over the twelve years that had passed. But it hadn't slipped out altogether. That she was being cared for by someone was enough to make our mom choke up with tears.

The next time Vani and I were home visiting our parents, I returned again to Mom's bed late at night. We snuggled against each other, shoulders touching underneath a thick comforter, bodies swallowed by the warmth. She turned her head and asked if Vani and her partner were serious. "Yes," I said. "They are." She asked if they would ever think of getting married. I laughed. I had anticipated that moment and I refused to answer. After a long period of silence, staring at the ceiling, toes wriggling under the covers, she moved on to another question. "Do you think Vani will introduce us to him?" In that moment I imagined Mom peeking out from curtains into Vani's world, wanting to feel closer to her daughter – just as I had when I was a kid. The question was one of many she had asked over the years that I couldn't answer. I couldn't speak for my sister. I was a mediator, a messenger, but if she was going to introduce her partner to Mom and Dad, it would be Vani's decision alone. I turned on my side to face Mom and said, "Why don't you ask Vani herself?"

The next few months were filled with conversations between Vani and Mom – conversations I didn't feel the need to mediate, and wasn't asked to. Five months later, Vani, her partner, Anand, and I piled on top of each other in an overnight Amtrak train from Penn Station in New York. We awoke south of Richmond. The train's diesel engine inched its way past heavy tree branches bending down by the windows, and within an hour we were at its final stop: Newport News, Virginia.

Dad picked us up from the train station, greeting all four of us with an enormous, toothy grin and tight hugs. On the ride home he chattered on about his upcoming research. Vani, Anand, and I were collapsed in the back seats after the overnight train ride, but Vani's partner, a secret science geek, leaned in and started asking Dad questions. Dad responded with his own geeky pleasure in explaining the experiment: his team would be launching a series of balloons to measure levels of aerosol in the upper atmosphere across the Indian Ocean. Despite our daze, we were all taken by the image of enormous balloons drifting off the coast of India towards Saudi Arabia, flying along with the monsoon.

During our trip, the four of us curled up on couches with Mom and Dad in the living room and played charades and silly word games late into the night. We ran along tree-lined trails and came home drenched in sweat, ready to throw back the cold fruit smoothies Mom had blended in her Vitamix. One late morning, on one of these scenic jogs that circled a large set of soccer fields, I heaved my way up a final incline before reaching the finish line and saw Vani's partner a couple dozen feet ahead of me. He wore a mischievous smile as he raced over and lifted Vani up off her feet just as she was catching her breath. They proceeded to dance across the parking lot to a tune that was only in his head. I caught Mom glancing at Vani and her partner with a deep, satisfied smile. Tears welled up in her eyes. I knew what she was noticing. The care and love they shared with each other. The kisses on the cheek, the spontaneous embraces.

Three days into our trip, as we were relaxing between spurts of activity, Mom pulled me into the kitchen, grabbed my arm, and pushed her smile into my face. I was startled and held my breath for what I was sure would be an uncomfortable question. "So, now that both you and Vani are not getting married but are living with partners…" I cringed. "I want to get you something," she continued. I looked into her eyes, searching for an explanation. What was this about? Where was she going with this? "You won't get any wedding gifts," she continued. I was sure this was turning into some guilt trip. "So I want to get each of you a Vitamix."

I paused and then snorted out a loud laugh and grabbed her for a squeeze. A Vitamix seemed like a ridiculous gesture, but one that was also full of reckless love. It was her way of saying that all of this was ok. It could become our new mediator. An object of care that could travel to places Mom couldn't be, that could nourish us, make our lives even a little bit easier.

I stole up to Vani's room, sat on the edge of her bed, and broke the news of our new kitchen appliances. We giggled, and then sat quietly and stared at each other in awe. Had we both stumbled into being good daughters without meaning to? Our parents had struggled to understand and reach both of us through these walls. None of this had been easy. And it wasn't as if this was the end. But just maybe Mom and Dad had come to accept the way happiness had taken shape in our lives.

What It Looks Like to Grow

Ankita Rao

The netting of the turquoise bridesmaid sari was stiff and unwieldy, and the petite woman wrapping it around me was dissatisfied when she finally tucked the pleats tightly under my belly button. She stood back and assessed as I pushed my shoulders back to stand taller.

"Your tummy scratches are showing," she said in a thick Indian accent, almost accusingly, as if there was anything I could do about the light white stretch marks trailing down my stomach like raindrops on a windowpane. They were unpretty, obvious marks, I knew, and Indians aren't known for being subtle. But I was still angry at the cold words she planted in my mind before I had to march down the aisle in front of hundreds of people at my friend's lavish wedding in Puerto Rico.

I've always been jealous of the people who get to wear their scars on the inside – the burden of their pain and experience tucked safely within skin and bone unless they decide to reveal what they've been through, what brought them to their low point that day, lying on the cold tile floor. And everyone has their cold tile floor – whether it's the darkness of a broken household, the lie that turned their tongue sharp, or an addiction they can't shake.

My scars, instead, are etched on the surface. They creep around my shoulders and on my hips and make me flinch if someone slides his hands under my shirt. In fitting rooms, on the new guy's couch, on the shores of a beach – that's where my story is forced to begin.

But for me it really begins sprawled naked on the floor in my bathroom when I was fourteen years old. I had come home from an afternoon run in the thick Florida summer and was peeling off my clothes when my head started to spin. Minutes later I heard a knock on the door, just conscious enough to be awash with horror as my father walked in to see why I wasn't responding. That was the first day it occurred to me that something was wrong.

☙

I grew up the feisty, anxious baby in an affectionate and open household on the white-washed coast of Florida. My parents – both hardworking immigrants from Hyderabad – never forced me or my older sister into activities or classes or career paths. Having experienced years of struggle, penny pinching, and heavy responsibility, my doctor father and yoga-teacher mother supported me as I hopped from the balance beam to karate to hip-hop dance class, buying me the appropriate shoes along the way. They paid for tutors if we lagged behind in classes, and enlisted me in a gifted program as soon as I passed the test in second grade. But if I brought home a B it was more of a "try harder next time" than the wrath that many of my other Indian American friends faced for second best.

But talking about how we felt, or saying "I love you" out loud, was rarely done in our home, a sunlit bungalow-type two-story on a river. My father was calm and introverted, and my mother light-hearted and practical. I was raised thinking that expressing feelings like this was formal, forced and stilted – an American practice that Danny Tanner espoused on *Full House* with his daughters, not us. We were too close, too sensible, to sit around dissecting our sadness. So when I slowly started to starve myself in ninth grade, they didn't say a word.

Some people know the exact reason why they developed an eating disorder – too much pressure or change or a big loss. For me it wasn't clear why, but I remember when. I remember going to watch a tennis tournament with my family in Miami and weighing myself on the hotel scale, something we never kept in our house – I had lost five pounds. I hadn't been trying to lose weight until then, and I was generally okay with my medium, curvy build. But I spent the rest of our weekend avoiding desserts and fries and felt a sort of high from feeling thinner. The seed had been watered.

I spent the coming days calculating calories to eat and miles to run. Occasionally I would daydream about boys and study for tests, but almost everything else revolved around numbers on the scale. I would come home from a seven-mile jog after school, sit on the floor for a hamstring stretch and fall asleep in that position, completely spent. My parents knew that I was losing weight, and they knew that I was obsessed with my running schedule, but they wrote it off as a health kick and waited for the phase to pass.

The next few months are almost inaccessible in my memory. When you're hungry the world actually becomes dimmer, the sounds a little softer. You don't seek intense sadness or anger – just a dull frustration that makes you short-tempered and aloof.

As the scale dipped from 115 pounds to 100 pounds to, eventually, 86 pounds, I figured that I was doing something right if nobody had stopped me yet. Ninth grade ended and I spent the summer in India, where my aunt told me I should model and I struggled to skip family meals and stick to my running routine under the unrelenting Hyderabad sun. But when I came back to start the next year of school, I was more determined than ever to feel my hipbones jutting under my skin. And then, that day on the cold tile floor arrived. And with it, humiliation, relief, and fear that my parents finally knew something was wrong.

"Just give her some protein bars," my pediatrician advised my mother when she took me to the doctor. We had made the appointment after my fainting spell and the Indian American doctor, a family friend, seemed less than concerned as she checked my weight, palpated my stomach, and sent me on my way. My mother was unsatisfied with her non-diagnosis and so we went home and continued as usual.

It took a while for me to accept that I was anorexic, or to even pair that word with my experience. Eating disorders were something I learned about in health class, from my friends, or in movies. These were rich, white people problems: Tracie Gold in an oversized sweater, some ballerina in Center Stage throwing up her food. My parents never talked about body image other than the occasional remarks about dieting – my mother is one of the few women I know who doesn't crash diet or make disparaging remarks about her own body with its spindly arms and legs or soft tummy. Worrying about the way you looked seemed like a luxury for people with too much time on their hands, and I was the superficial daughter who couldn't get over herself.

But by the time I diagnosed myself, with the help of some friends who had experienced this themselves, something strange happened: I started eating.

It was the middle of track season in tenth grade when I lost what I thought was control. I was at a family party in New Jersey and I devoured a bowl of cocktail peanuts on the table, and suddenly there were no more rules. On one day I would run, although by this time I was constantly getting injured and slowed down by shin splints and muscle tears, and try to stick with my eating plan. The next day I would chase spoonfuls of peanut butter with Coke and then lie on my bed feeling like the ugliest girl in the world.

My body changed quickly – I gained weight every week as I struggled to figure out what it meant to eat like a normal person. By the end of the school year, the numbness of hunger and routine had completely slipped away and I was left with something far more difficult: pain.

I cried all the time: in my closet when I gave away another pair of tight pants, in fitting rooms at the mall, and on the chaise in our living room when I screamed to my parents that I hated my body. They weren't sure how to respond to this new twist. My dad would tell me to stick to a more consistent diet plan, and my mom, the youngest of seven siblings, told me to toughen up. The body, thin or fat, she said, was just a vehicle for intellect and experiences. It didn't warrant quite so much angst.

And so I forced my way through high school without answers. I was lively and social with my friends, and a decent student in my advanced academic program. I went to dances (having a small breakdown every time I bought a dress), and tried alcohol for the first time at my friend Brittany's house. I got my license and drove to the beach at night to watch silver-crested waves make their way to the shore. But I couldn't shake this part of me, and in ways that were no longer displayed across my ribs and collarbones, I got worse.

I turned to binging and purging – throwing up secretly in my bathroom and cleaning the toilet bowl immediately. I stopped eating normal meals altogether and continued to swing between dieting and desserts until I weighed almost forty pounds more than when I had started high school. When I got my admission letters for college the first thing I thought was: I hope I lose weight before my first day.

In the second semester of my freshman year at the University of Florida I did something no one in my family had ever done: I went to therapy.

There was nothing dramatic about my first day of therapy with Roberta Seldman, a poised psychologist with a salt-and-pepper bob who nodded with equal parts empathy and the experience of having heard hundreds of people tell a somewhat similar story. After that she asked me to supplement my appointments with a group therapy session that met every Tuesday in the basement of the health center. And it was here – under ugly fluorescent lights – that I met a group of women that taught me what it meant to thrive.

In the early days of therapy – almost four years into having some sort of evolving eating disorder – I faked it. I read the suggested books and went to see a nutritionist to track my eating habits. I put together the right, eloquent sentences, and used the right words. But I couldn't access the part of me that still dictated what I ate or how I looked at myself in the mirror. I knew how to cry, but more out of anger than catharsis or grief. Without any practice with feelings and emotions, I felt strange taking time to talk about myself in a group, as if I was stealing time from the girls who were still in the throes of anorexia, thin and gaunt and listless.

My parents supported me through this in the same way they did when I tried a new activity – observing, without too much intervention, and footing the bills when I needed to pay for a costly nutritionist and out-of-network therapist. And because we had spent years without discussion or labeling what they still didn't see as a disease, I decided to involve them in every step. I called them during particularly dark days from my dorm room and sent them the cathartic notes I scribbled during a moment of clarity.

Sometimes they didn't get it. During a visit home one day I took a walk with my mom and explained to her why I couldn't try to lose weight and recover at the same time. By then my weight was higher than it had been most of my life, and she couldn't quite grasp the idea that I wasn't actively trying to diet. "I'm okay with this for now," I said about my body, an idea that I didn't actually believe but was trying to accept. "I'd be okay if you were a little thinner," she said with a small laugh, a laugh that stayed stuck at my core for days.

It took months, even years, of watching the girls in therapy – most of them high-achieving, driven students – break down crying in the group sessions to understand that I couldn't intellectualize what had happened to me and still expect to be fixed. And so, during my junior year of college, and in the same basement room, I broke down.

That day I cried loud and out loud. I cried out of anger – at my parents, for not forcing me to get help earlier, at the culture that forced me to value myself based on a scale, and the boys who liked me more when my ribs were showing. And I cried to grieve. For the days and years I had given away to this disease – the thousands of happy moments overshadowed by a desire to be skinny and numb. For the girl who didn't feel beautiful for more than a few seconds at a time, and who needed attention like water to make up for that void. I cried because even after seven years of living with an eating disorder, I still had no faith that I would ever be normal again.

"I've been waiting for that," Roberta said when I was done. I went back to my room across campus and slept for hours.

After that, there was no stitching up my newly opened wound, as ugly as it could be. If my parents even hinted at exasperation, or still wanting me to lose weight and become my average, pre-anorexic self, I no longer allowed their comments to cycle through my mind and steep for days, I just told them that it wasn't okay. I yelled when they made flippant jokes, or the time they hid a batch of cookies that I baked from me when I came home. "In India everyone makes fun of each other," my mother would say, shaking her head at my sensitivity.

One day my father, who had recently sent me a diet book written by Martina Navratilova, commented that I needed to find a consistent workout (I had never stopped exercising) to maintain my weight. I slammed the door and sped to the gym in my little red car, refusing to answer my phone or tell anyone where I was going. He, my mom, and my sister showed up to check if I was okay, forcing me to leave my elliptical machine and meet them in the parking lot.

"How dare you," I shouted at him. "After all these years. After ignoring everything I've been through. Now you think you can fucking tell me what to do with my body?"

Cursing in front of my parents, let alone at my parents, was not done in my house. We weren't even allowed to say "shut up" growing up, and talking back was one of the lowest forms of communication. But there was something that shifted when I started to look closely at myself, and who I wanted to be, and it changed the way my parents and I interacted. I wasn't normally that fiery or disrespectful, but I started to recognize that all four of us had allowed this part of ourselves to go undeveloped – the part of us that didn't know how to express what we were going through, allowing that pain or anger to culture and spread until some sort of implosion.

For me, this realization also meant my parents didn't always know what was best for me. This was something I needed to actively figure out myself.

৵

In the coming years I would test that theory of who I was meant to be. I trekked through Brazil and Central America and India with a backpack and open eyes. I moved to India twice. The first time, I lived in a slum community and worked on a development project with a hundred kids, and I spent the year connecting with women who were trying to figure out how to feed their families. I recognized their hunger – as different as it was from mine – and felt a sort of empathy I didn't know I had. The second time I moved, I left a perfectly comfortable job and life in Washington, DC, to work as a freelance journalist across several Indian states, traveling to tribal areas where I couldn't speak the language or access a policeman.

None of this was easy on my parents, especially my mom, who would call me after reading violent headlines about rape and rioting, begging me to come home. But it was something I needed to do after I had spent so many years trapped and limited by this strange, static disease. In India I found a new strength in my body that made me both powerful and insignificant amid a sea of brown bodies that looked like me. My insecurity, my battle with my stomach and arms and thighs, was threatened by a new type of vibrant connection to the world, a sense of purpose I had never known.

I always thought recovering from an eating disorder was a finite journey that would look a certain way – maybe ending in a strong, fit body and a normal, stable diet. Instead, at age twenty-seven, it has meant understanding the texture and breadth of this disease in intimate detail. Practicing hours of yoga to understand the pulses in my wrists and temples, the rise and fall of my abdomen with each deep breath. Eating food in a way that makes me feel calm and grounded.

That healing process hasn't just been about me. My family and I have become the kind of people who talk about feelings. We cry at the dinner table and sit patiently through each other's outbursts, when they happen. We ask questions when we know that something is missing in the silence. In the years that followed my first day in therapy, every single person in my house has seen a psychologist or sought treatment for something they once tried to tuck away and ignore. And no matter how difficult it gets – and at times it has gotten very tough – we work hard to let go of some of the burden we were trying to bear alone.

❧

On a hot Mumbai morning, just a few weeks ago, I stood in front of the mirror in a bra and underwear after a cold bucket bath, my arms akimbo like Superwoman. I gazed without flinching at the stretch marks on my stomach, aggressively protecting myself from any harsh words that tried to float in my mind. After a while, a long while, I felt like I had stepped out of my body and was looking down at the girl who couldn't have met herself eye-to-eye just a few years ago.

And from this angle all I could think was that the scars were there for a reason – to remind me what it looks like to grow.

Breathe

Phiroozeh Petigara

On the day we arrived in Canada, my father gathered up his Pakistani-ness with one hand, his Parsi-ness with the other, and pulled them up over our heads like a shroud. We settled into our new country thus – under the veil of the old.

✧

The apartment is small, dark, and smells like paint. Mummy and Daddy are tucking my younger sister, Fiona, and I into our new twin beds bought at a discount furniture store. Someone must have told them that this is what you do in Canada, along with no littering and no honking when you drive.

"I want to go back to Karachi," I beg, eyes on Mummy.

"Give it time," she says, stroking my hair.

"I won't eat until you let me go back."

They laugh. I say this every night and by morning, I'm starving. Worse, in Canada, you eat Bran Flakes for breakfast, and I hate them. The dark brown flakes scratch my throat. I fish out the raisins and make a necklace on the rim of my bowl while the cereal turns to a gray mush. Daddy scolds Mummy to scold me to eat.

Before Daddy turns out the light, he says, "Good night, sleep tight, and don't forget, marry a nice Parsi boy."

I giggle. "I'm only eleven. I'm too young to marry."

"When you marry, you will marry a Parsi." He turns off the light and follows Mummy out.

Squeezing my eyes shut, I conjure Karachi: the humid air that leaves my palms ever-moist, my best friends and I playing hide-and-seek every evening after tuitions, the cool reprieve of Nani and Nana's air-conditioned bedroom where I spend most nights. I imagine I'm snuggled up on the silky brown sofa at the foot of their bed, my grandparents' steady breathing lulling me to sleep.

I stare at the white walls of my new Canadian room, nauseated by the smell of new paint. Beside me, Fiona is already asleep and doesn't hear me cry.

&

My heart pounds as I take the stairs two at a time up to Nani-Nana's flat on the third floor. I'm sweating so much from playing I have to change my T-shirt. It is the month before my parents get the news that our application to immigrate to Canada has been accepted, and I'm thoroughly enjoying my Pakistani childhood. Everyone's out this evening: my big group of friends plays hide-and-seek all over the five-building compound, the older boys play cricket on the volleyball court, the teenagers sit on the bench in the shadows. I push Nani's front door with the weight of my body – it's never locked – and slip undetected past the grown-ups enjoying drinks on the balcony and hurry to the back of the apartment. From Nani's cupboard, I pull out a clean T-shirt from the shelf reserved for my clothes. I touch the inside of the cupboard door. Nani had her handyman attach a piece of wood so that I can play teacher-teacher properly. The chalk writes so smoothly on the soft surface, I feel like a real teacher, just like Nani.

In the bathroom, I squeeze sweat from my sadra. I had my navjote last year, and at first it was fun to wrap the kasti around my waist, back and forth and back again, just like the grownups did every morning and evening, whispering their prayers under their breath. But now I often forget to do my sadra-kasti, and, when I do remember, the kasti always feels so tight around my waist. Once in a while, Daddy forces me to do it in front of him and I mumble the prayers softly because I've already forgotten some of the words.

I race back downstairs eager to join back in the game. Whenever I'm the seeker, Nani gets complaints from the neighbors, "That granddaughter of yours has the loudest voice in the compound." I jump over the three steps onto the ground floor landing and freeze. Daddy's car has pulled up in front of Nani's building. My heart sinks.

"Chal, Phiroozeh, the new round is beginning," my best friend calls.

Biting my lip to keep it from quivering, I slip into the backseat. I'm dying to spend the night at Nani-Nana's but I know the rules: sleepovers on weekends and during the summer only. None of my friends live in my compound, and my parents' flat is always quiet.

As Daddy drives away, I look out the back seat window as my friends start a new game of hide-and-seek.

ॐ

"Phi, there's a boy on the phone asking for you. You don't want to talk to him, do you?" Mum sounds aghast.

I remove the compress from my head, stumble to the kitchen, squinting against the rare sunlight in rainy Vancouver.

It's Marcus Yates. I've been in love with him since grade nine. "I noticed you weren't in Biology all week. I thought you might want to know the homework." Marcus Yates is calling me. At my house. I sink onto the kitchen chair drinking in his beautiful Aussie accent as he goes on about paramecium or bacteria or whatever.

When the shit hits the fan some months later, Dad stands in my room, his large body taking up all the space.

"I told you, Parsis marry Parsis," he shouts.

"Woah, Dad, he just asked me to go on a walk."

His voice grows louder. "Don't think you are like the goras that you can talk back to your father. You are 17. You are too young for dating."

"My friends have been dating since they were 12."

"Your friends are *Canadian*."

"*I* am Canadian," I laugh through my tears.

"We are from Pakistan," he shouts, "We are Parsi. We are respectable. We are not like the goras who –"

I tune him out as he repeats the same thing he's been yelling at me for months. I look to Mum, pleading with my eyes, but she stands quietly in the corner staring at the carpet. After Dad leaves, I cry into my pillow, my eardrums vibrating from his shouts. In my school life, I am in my senior year and being asked to cast votes for "cutest couple." In my home life, I am expected to go from adolescence to matrimony. My high school class is mostly white and I have no immigrant friends to help make sense of the discord in my life.

Mum comes to my bed, stroking my arm, which only makes me cry harder. I sink into the comfort of her touch.

"You know he's being unfair," I say. I want her to be like the TV mums, raising an eyebrow and giving their husbands what-for when they're being silly. I want so badly for her to take my side. "Mum, please. It's not like Marcus is in a biker gang. He's on the honor roll. He has the second highest GPA in our entire class. You sat with his mum at the band concert. You liked her, remember?"

With her hand on mine, she says, "He's your father, jaan."

It is the first time I see where the loyalties lie in this family. Mum says it's Our Way, to obey one's father. But I am 17, in the blushes of my first love, and did I mention, Canadian? My friends do what they want, when they want. The thing that hurts the most, that sends shards of pain down my body is that she, my mother, is one half of this parenthood – does her opinion count for nothing?

It is a fight I will never win, a rule that will never make sense in my Canadianized mind: in our family, it is my father who rules the household and his scepter is green, topped with a crescent moon and star.

❧

At 20, the shroud my father has held over me for so long is suddenly, and without warning, lifted. My mother simply says I am now allowed to date. I am floored. Are they tired of fighting me? Do they want me to have one last hurrah before carting in my hand-picked groom? I don't know, and I don't ask. But under the protective shroud, there is no scaffolding, no foundation, no way to understand or navigate my sudden freedom. I have no concept of the opposite gender, how to talk to them, how to relate to them, how to value myself around them. The message I have internalized was: I would be lucky to be chosen.

My parents continue to "find me boys." Parsi women are calling my parents because at twenty-five, I am almost at my expiration date and saving me from spinsterhood is now a community project. My dates with Parsis are sometimes hilarious, often painful. It hurts to contort myself into the teeny tiny box I'm asked to squeeze myself into.

"The shorts you wore the other day were really short," says one guy. "It didn't look nice."

Another, when I mention backpacking across South America, enthuses, "Oh, I also love to travel. I've gone on several cruises to the Bahamas, the Caribbean, Mexico…"

One is particularly pushy. "Look, I think two weeks of chatting on the phone is more than enough time for you to decide whether or not to fly to

Chicago and visit me. There are a *lot* of women I'm talking to. You have to decide whether you're serious about this or I'll have to move on."

I picture a shelf in his apartment lined with mason jars, each containing a prospective wife. Every night, he examines each jar, turning it this way and that, assessing the properties of each specimen. Childrearing hips? Check. Traditional? Most definitely. Dhansak skills? Not quite like Mummy's.

I know I don't belong on that shelf. But it still hurts to be rejected by someone I never chose. To be dumped by a man I've never met before ever having had a boyfriend.

જ

When I return from a year abroad in London at the end of my twenty-fifth year, my parents beg me to attend the Zoroastrian Youth Congress, a notoriously thinly-veiled attempt to get Parsis to marry within the community. I have avoided them since my first one at sixteen, when I'd been hit on by disturbingly old men, and had sworn off Congresses forever. Why, then, do I agree? Because my friends from London are coming. Because the beaches of Miami sound better than a Vancouver winter.

So here I am at a Parsi speed dating event in a stuffy conference room, willing the walls to collapse around me. I came because I thought it would be entertaining. Instead, it's riling me up in ways I don't quite understand. The guy sitting across from me in matching beige pants and short-sleeved shirt must be close to forty. His careful comb-over consists of three strands of hair pulled optimistically over his shiny pate. The way his ankle rests on the opposite knee reminds me of my father.

"So, how many dishes can you cook?"

I burst out laughing. He does not join me.

I look around at the guys in the room. Am I really expected to marry someone based solely on the fact that he's Parsi? I remember Dad saying this as he tucked us in when I was a child. He didn't explain the importance then, he doesn't explain it now, but the expectation stands.

I don't entirely blame my parents. Theirs was an arranged marriage. By my generation, things have advanced. You can have an "introduction," where you're introduced to someone by a family friend and have full freedom to date them for at least a couple of months before getting married. There are also social gatherings such as this Congress, where you can meet someone entirely on your own, in this carefully orchestrated Parsi parade, and marry them a few months later, a year tops.

I know all this, yet I don't identify with any of it. I'm too far gone, too Canadian. I want to date. Marriage is not a priority; at best, it's a distant possibility. I'm here for the warmth, I remind myself, though I am beginning to wonder if there are easier ways to access a beach vacation.

The next guy to sit across me is young and cocky. I dated a few of those. Cocky guys, horny guys, snoringly boring guys. Guys who were just guys but who were elevated to god status because they were Parsi.

"I like armadillos, do you?" he asks, slumping back in his chair. I am relieved to see his note paper, which we were all handed upon entrance, is also blank.

"I prefer iguanas."

I relax into an inane discussion, a much welcome break from the wife auditions. I think of the iguanas that roamed free in Trinidad. The heat in the air, my friends all around, the freedom in my lungs. South Korea then London, same thing: a life I'd carved out for myself, the giddy feeling of freedom in faraway places. I was supposed to go to Italy next.

So why are you here instead, Phiroozeh? Because at twenty-five, I am an outcast. Choosing literature and wanderlust over marriage and children is something no one understands. Even my own friends, born and raised in Canada, are getting married and having babies, encouraging me to do the same. I am the third wheel, the fifth wheel, the seventh wheel, the girl for whom a chair is attached to the end of the table at restaurants, bumped by passing waiters throughout the evening.

So instead of Italy, here I am in Miami. To see what normal feels like.

It's itchy.

"How often do you do your sadra-kasti?" asks the next guy.

I look around for the Candid Camera crew. Obviously this is a joke – no one says these things in real life.

"I think the last time was when I was about fifteen? Or was it fourteen?" I sit back and savor the color drain from his face. He scribbles furiously on his note paper.

Despite the private mirth, my stomach curdles. I feel stupid. What am I doing here? Why do I subject myself to these private humiliations?

I thought at the very least the Congress would feed that long-ago thirst to know my religion and culture more deeply. I had always wanted connection, a sense of belonging, a true understanding of what it meant to be Parsi and Zoroastrian. In the religion classes I'd attended as a teen, all the questions I had about the faith were left unanswered by adults only interested in having us memorize prayers. At the Congress, one panel I attend, meant to discuss the

Gathas, the Zoroastrian sacred texts, ends up being instead a recital of some of its passages. No discussion, no explanation. It's the religion I've grown up with as presented by my father, and here it is again, religion as showmanship, as outward accouterments.

The next guy to sit across from me is cute. I saw him on the airport shuttle to the hotel, thought he was a hot Italian. Turns out, he's Parsi with a tan, from California.

"How's this going?" he asks, gesturing to the note paper in my lap, covered in doodles.

"I've found a husband. We're getting married in the gazebo at sunset."

He laughs. My fists unclench.

৵

Dad invites me to coffee when I visit Vancouver. He asks about California, where I've been living for three years now, about my writing, the research I'm doing about Pakistan and Parsis, offers insight about our family. I am elated. Finally, a real conversation with my father, finally I'm good enough.

He leans forward. "So, when are you guys having kids?"

I am shocked. "I just got married. To a Parsi. When will you stop harassing me?"

His face lights up. "You don't know the order of things? After marriage, there is a child," he counts on his finger. "Then the second child. Then doing your children's navjote ceremony so they can be proper Parsis, then getting the children married. To nice Parsi boys, don't forget," he laughs. "It never ends."

There it is. My life preordained. The weight of it settles on my chest. The hurt of it lingers.

৵

"Tea?" Mum asks as I enter the kitchen. She strokes my arm. It feels like a trail of fire, her touch burns my skin so. I've been in California for seven years but things with my parents haven't become easier. I agree, hoping my reluctance isn't obvious, knowing it is. She moves quietly about the kitchen and I sit at the dining table checking Facebook.

The kitchen is crammed with photos, photos I never look at directly but which imprint themselves onto my brain nonetheless. Sharlene as a one year old, born a year after we arrived in Canada. Mum in her dragon-boating uniform, paddle in the air. Fiona and Sharlene snowboarding. Mum at her sixtieth birthday, standing with Sharlene and Fiona, arms around each other, heads thrown back in laughter. Mum's touch doesn't seem to burn my sisters' skin.

The rest of the kitchen is crammed with photos of Fiona's new baby, the first grandchild in the family. Blown-up photos line every windowsill, counter, and cabinet. Fiona did not marry a Parsi boy. She did the worst thing a Parsi can do according to my parents, and married a – gasp – Muslim. But then Fiona had a baby and all was forgiven.

"Phi, I wanted to tell you, you should look into publishing in Canada," Dad has joined us in the kitchen. My chest tightens, my guard comes up. Just this morning, he left an article on my bed: "Women over 35, increased chances of risky pregnancies." I crumpled it up with shaking hands and threw it into the garbage can without reading it.

I sit rigid, wary, waiting. Mum pours the tea and I check the clock. It's only been eight minutes.

She and I sat in the same spot in the kitchen when she took her turn, a year after Dad's interrogation, asking me, begging me to have children.

"It's different for me," I said, wanting her to really hear my words, to understand. "I don't hear a biological clock, I hear the revving of a jumbo jet flying me to my next destination. For other women, smelling a newborn sets off a bell inside them. For me, it's the smell of a new notebook, seeing a new story unfold. Does that make sense?"

She waved away my words. Children were life's greatest joy, not all this art and traveling. I could do those later. The true work of a woman was to give. To her husband. To her children. That was the essence of life.

It was then that I realized the full extent of my error. My parents wore western clothes and spoke fluent English. They spent several summers at French camp with Sharlene. Mum was dragon-boating, having potlucks with her white friends. All this reeked of well-adjusted. If my mum had been like the Punjabi aunties in Little India, wearing shalwar kameez and making fresh roti with every meal, it would have taken me half as long to figure out. You can take the Desi out of the Desh, you can put them in jeans, in a dragon boat, in a tent, but you cannot, for the life of you, shake their deeply entrenched beliefs.

"He must be missing you," Dad says.

My Parsi husband. The one photo of me on the fridge is with him, at our wedding. It's taken from a faraway angle, we're both smiling for someone else's camera. "I should go call him before bed."

"Thanks for hanging out," says Mum.

"Good-night, jaan," says Dad.

I leave the kitchen, breathing into the tightness still lodged in my chest.

My bedroom is scattered with vestiges of my youth. *The Norton Anthology of English Literature*, my first attempts at oil painting, beaten-up Lonely Planet guides. I sit on the twin bed bought twenty-five years ago when we first moved to Canada.

The tears begin right on cue. Deep remorse at the still-fractured relationship with my parents. Sadness that at thirty-five, my life is everything I want it to be but in their eyes, it will never be complete, *I* will never be complete.

A text from California, my good friend checking in. The first person I met who writes all day, who is childless by choice. In this little corner of California that I've carved out for myself, for the first time in my life, I am not alone. For the first time, I am in a place where my choices are valid, valued.

I wipe my face. The hurt of my past will dim over time. For now, the present, which I have fought so hard to create, is mine for the taking.

I text back: "I fly back Sunday night. Let's write together Monday."

She responds immediately: "Great. 10am, the usual spot."

The tightness in my chest loosens. I can breathe again.

Amma

Hema Sarang-Sieminski

When I was twenty-eight, I wore pink taffeta and jewels and a painted face that smiled and smiled and smiled. I married a tender-hearted boy from Kolkata while my partner watched and we laughed and laughed. We were two brides to the gay queen, his lesbo sidekicks. We felt as if we had won. We felt as if we could do anything. Finally, we would be free to do and live as we pleased and everyone would be happy – the three of us, and my parents, at last. Sometimes one of us couldn't laugh, but I would rally the troops because there was no room for sadness, not now, and this would be over soon.

It was a large affair. Three celebrations. Kolkata. Chennai. Framingham, MA. But my mother was not happy. She barely looked up.

One

I am Tamil where growing up Tamil meant Hood Buttermilk, Colombo Yogurt, and sticky white rice with Cape Cod potato chips. Chutney powder was sprinkled on the side and old cassettes of Roja played in the background. In the summertime, during school vacation, it was Indian jasmine in my long braids and cool, dark temples with elephants that would exchange bananas for blessings as I entered. We listened to stories and overheard family gossip while sitting on my grandmother's kitchen swing eating banana leaf plates of parupu sadam and rasam and nai that seeped through our fingers and dribbled onto our laps when we tried to eat with our American-born hands.

My father (Inyengar) and mother (Iyer) met in a chemistry lab in Chennai when they were 32 and 24. The minor differences in the religious preferences of their families made their marriage deeply controversial for 1975 Trichy and Sri Rangam, but my mother's threats to end her life with cyanide at the lab and my father's job prospects in the US led to familial consent. They would move to Washington, DC, a few months later. I don't know much about their life in the US before we were born, but I always wondered if it was as lonely as it was cold in DC for brown folks with accents and long names that first winter of their migration. I was born in Cleveland, Ohio, in 1978. I was their first child. I was their daughter.

Two

I want to tell you what it was like before I learned my heart couldn't stay open anymore. I was a good girl wanting to love and to please and to be loved. I was good at it, though loving that hard comes with a price. I paid it over and over again.

Like a good Tamil Hindu Brahmin girl, I learned long division before I started kindergarten. I wore Harvard T-shirts. I was polite and considerate. I wanted to be a doctor. I already knew meat was murder. I was only going to marry the boy my parents told me I could marry. I thought dating was immoral. I thought drugs and alcohol equaled death. I knew it was my duty to keep my parents happy. At school, I was a very shy but smart brown kid in an almost exclusively white public school. I had unfortunate mother-chosen fashion and hardly ever talked except when answering teachers' questions frequently and correctly. I had few friends, though we didn't talk about the loneliness of racism then. Friends, according to my parents, especially American friends, could be "bad influences" or "distractions" anyway. I didn't talk back too much. I aced my homework and tests and only cried sometimes when my dad wasn't looking after he'd give me Volume Library Encyclopedia reading assignments on Sunday mornings. I began Karnatic music voice lessons when I was five years old and was adequately awkward and embarrassed, yet cooperative and talented, when asked to sing spontaneously in community and family gatherings. And each night, I would say four prayers to Ganesh, Saraswati, Shiva, and Lakshmi, to keep me good, and to keep my mom and dad and brother and grandparents and everyone and everything else in the world safe and alive and happy always. My parents loved me. I loved them. We were an orthodox, noble, god-fearing family with centuries of traditional Indian values behind us. That's what we all grew up with, right?

That's part of the story, the part that has been the hardest to see through.

Three

Unlike many other good Tamil-American little girls born to South Asian immigrants in the US, I learned real young that my mother wouldn't just die for me, but that she could die because of me. Her death would come because of what I felt, what I did, what I didn't, what I dreamed, who I was, and who I was not. And my father, well he would just stand by and watch until he himself, overcome with grief, would also die.

Moms, especially our South Asian Ammas, are supposed to be all-loving and all-knowing even when we're exasperated with them. Overbearing at times, but always from a place of love. Intrusive at times, but for our own good. Overprotective, but only because they worry so much about us. No one likes to talk about moms, abusive moms, who hurt their children. No one likes to talk about moms with untreated mental illness. No one likes to hear about moms who are incestuous. No one wants to hear about moms who need their daughters to be too close. She was never Amma to me.

I always called her Mom. On the outside, Mom was the short-statured, mildly overweight, quiet portrait of hard-won professional success, maternal sacrifice, middle-class prosperity, piousness, and community leadership with the occasional egotistical streak of temper or adamancy that could be mistaken as the mark of a free-spirit. Her birthday was on Valentine's Day. Her name stems from the Sanskrit word for "peace." The irony is sometimes overwhelming.

On the inside, she was violent in very dark ways. My father never heard or intervened even when he was standing right there. I was a sensitive one with tears never very far away. Mom liked to have a sensitive little girl who would cry for her until it looked like the prettiest expression of feminine love from a creature she could have and hurt. Mom loved tears when they were for her and hated them when they weren't. And Mom hurt very deeply when she hated. She held my heart in her hands and took pleasure in the pain she inflicted. That was, above all, the deepest and most enduring part of her abuse.

Mom felt enraged and betrayed when I wanted space. She would explode with anger that would make me shake and retreat in tears to my room and moments later she would act as if nothing at all had happened. By day she would carve my pre-adolescent, adolescent, and adult body to pieces with her eyes and touch and words assessing what belonged where, what didn't belong and what was abnormal, masculine, or obscene. In the wake of her ferocity were waves of self-hatred for her role in the development of my body. She would pound her own forehead with her fist shaking in sobs, and I would make her feel better telling her how much I loved her, telling her I was sorry, and that I would be better because I, *I* had made her ill with worry.

She would share my twin bed with me most nights until I was in high-school and even after that sometimes. Mom would tell me she would die if I didn't want her there. She had chest pains, and could die in her sleep. I was selfish if I didn't want her to be there. Selfish girls want their moms to die, but I didn't want my mom to die. Not because of me. In the evenings or sometimes before bedtime, she'd call me to my room where she preferred to rest and would plead for my touch, my words, my love. I would hold my breath quiet and stroke her hair, rub her back, legs, thighs, and feet hoping she would forget it was me who was there. Me, the daughter who made her ill, the daughter who made her feel so much rage. When I would try to leave while she was still calm she would plead for me, bless me, tell me god would bless me, that I was her darling, her best daughter, if I could stay longer and that she would die if I didn't. I would stay until Mom would notice she had a captive recipient of her leading questions, distortions, and rage.

She was the wielder of these sorts of daily demands disguised as disciplines. It was all for my own good, of course. Every good daughter wished for the happiness of her parents. Only those who love you will tell you the truth about you. Everyone else will just laugh behind your back. That's what she used to say. I don't know her childhood history. Sometimes I wish I did so I could understand more about how it is that she became so wounded. And other times, I just don't care.

On the inside, I would go away. I would disappear into my room during the free hours I had before anyone was home or noticed I had my door closed, but not locked, because our doors never had locks. I would disappear into inarticulate and inaccessible worlds of sexual violence, pain, and a deep longing for comfort, safety, and love. There, in these fantasies of suffering and love, I would turn to a woman spirit I would come to name my protectoress. She was somehow also me. In these dark day and night dreams that would play on endless repeat, she would hold my broken body and heart without question and remove pain if only for a few seconds.

And this was all before I knew I was queer.

Four

I started looking for gay husbands when I was nineteen years old. I came out as gay to myself when I was fourteen years old. It wasn't terrifying – not yet. I just wanted to be a feminist activist in San Francisco in an apartment with a balcony, a cat, a typewriter, and a lover who was a girl. I fell in love with feminism. I scoured libraries for faded stories from the sixties and seventies of mass demonstrations for peace and justice, *Ms. Magazine*, NOW, Gloria Steinem, and even Betty Friedan. I fell in love with the voices of women speaking their truths and making the personal political. I was drawn to the power in the voices of survivors decades before I would discover my own. I was still going to be a doctor. But now, maybe a psychologist or a journalist too.

When I was fifteen, I met out, LGBTQ-identified women and men for the first time at a summer camp near Boston, where I grew up, that my parents accidentally sent me to thinking it would be an educational pre-college experience. It was truly very educational. I came back each day that summer even surer that I was gay, didn't want to go to school near home, and didn't want to be a doctor anymore. Home felt like living in a cage after that summer. I was counting down to college and the freedom it promised. Mom could sense my distance, my sense of self, my growth, and my longing for life. She was determined to snuff that out. I came home one day and found a note on the kitchen table that was signed "Not your mother." She had read my journals. My father demanded to see the pages scrawled with my very first words about my newly found sexuality. She was cold with rage in her voice and had hard hands that coated me with shame. My father did not look at me for months as I begged him to let me be his daughter again. A year later, I would call Philadelphia, with the more distant and lesser known Ivy, home.

By eighteen I was out and queer on campus. I found love and friendship I had never known in a community of feminist activists. We had keys to the Women's Center and held meetings late at night talking about sexism and fraternities, sexual violence, the construction of gender, reproductive justice, hairy legs, Adrienne Rich, and Audre Lorde. That was the summer I went home to work with Boston NOW and to celebrate feminism, freedom, adulthood, and the end of an era of shy and scared.

I saw a classmate from high school at Boston Pride that summer. It was my first Pride, and I was marching with Boston NOW, holding the banner up front, chanting loud and proud. I was feminist, fierce, and marching for justice and visibility while dodging photographers in case I ended up on the evening news. Melissa ran out from the sidelines. We hadn't spoken before. When we were in high school, she was out, pariah, and younger. I was the shy brown kid. Now we were both queer in Boston.

I got caught on the telephone that night telling her when I first knew. I remember my stomach falling when I realized my mother had been listening in on our conversation. I got off the phone quickly. I barely knew her. I had just wanted connection – another queer in Walpole, MA. Melissa didn't get that I was unsafe and couldn't run into the woods behind the middle school to have afternoon sex with her because I had scarier things to worry about.

I remember Ani's "Not a Pretty Girl" playing on repeat for the nineteenth time. I remember my mother pounding on the door so hard it strained against the dresser I had propped up in front of it. She banged her head hard against the wall over and over again, wailing like she had lost a loved one. A lover, perhaps. Not quite a daughter. Instead of spreading righteous eighteen-year-old slightly outdated feminist rage that summer, I was on lock-down. This was before everyone had cell phones. I was alone. I stayed in my bedroom until no one was around. I was scared. I lost my breath. I lost my voice. Time away in India at a spiritual youth convention would fix me, or so my parents thought. I spent the rest of that summer praying for a solution at an ashram in Puttaparthi, India, and was blessed to find friendship and support. I returned home. I was forced to promise I was straight. It bought me time.

Five

I met my wife when I was nineteen. We fell in love fast and strong and she helped me remember how to play. We wandered the streets laughing at the attitude of berries and loving dinners together that were beyond our means, finding small objects that were perfect for pocket charms and clouds that looked like animals sometimes. She was color and light and I clung hard. I held on hard, and you don't hold onto love that hard, so I learn. Now.

I was doing thesis work on queer women's movements in India, and Mumbai that following summer of 1999 was beautiful. I met brown dykes and brown fags for what felt like the first time living and breathing and loving in the land that I barely know but is imprinted in my blood. I felt brown and beautiful and full of life. There was wholeness there and a healing of pieces of myself that had seemed impossible. My girl came to visit me for ten days. We sat on the balcony of the YWCA hostel until 4 AM with conversations that kept blooming in the jasmine-scented night air. We lay naked in our twin beds pushed together. We were alive.

I came home after that summer. My mother was instantly suspicious and disturbed by the India that had made her daughter so radiant and happy. I, however, felt powerful. I felt strong. I felt beautiful. I felt like I had found a homeland that I did not know existed for me, in me.

I was home for barely an afternoon before that world, that homeland, was gone. There was a panic so deep within me I wanted to run across the ocean back to the land that had held me so close less than thirty hours ago in its warm brown arms. There was rage in Tamil and English and my memories don't hold these words anymore. It was summertime in Walpole, MA, and I was suddenly cold and hot and wet-faced and scared. I did not want this now. Not now.

My mother held the soft red parchment of my journal in her hands. I tore it away from her. She had read enough. My father too. Their hands were violent. They used words that felt contorted and vile, twisting my love, my community, me into something unrecognizable – something inhuman. I stood before them shaking, trying to keep my voice as they read it. They called my words, my feelings, disgusting. I felt paralyzed. I think something died in me that day. They turned my girl into a demon. They turned love letters to venom. They turned reflections on the pain and beauty of gay male sex workers in dingy bars, their eyes sad, but spirits intact, for now, into dirty stories of whores and sinners.

I lived in a vacuum for the rest of summer. I could not leave or speak without their permission. I sat in my head, in agony. When desperation set in, I decided to do whatever I could to go home. My home. My girl picked me up in a red rental car and we made our getaway to Philadelphia. As a condition to my plea to leave, I was forced to write a letter, and swear before God, that I would never hurt my parents again. They took this as a pledge of my reform. The small child in me held this as a vow to never cause my parents pain. I tried not to, ever again.

I think there was a beginning of healing, a beginning of growth that somehow ended that summer. There was something new and hard in its place. I had written earlier that summer, "If home is really where the heart is, then I am a fault, the line of rupture, my heart torn in two."

I'm not quite sure how, but I kept building from that spot forward and I never looked back. The spaces within my heart got wider and wider until I almost broke apart. But I didn't. Not quite.

I remember I was working at the Penn Women's Center one afternoon when I posted a message on AMLAG (Arranged Marriage for Lesbians and Gays) – a website for South Asian queers looking for marriages in desperation. It was 1999. I posted to the group: "Out 19 year old lesbian South Asian (Tamil Brahmin) girl seeking gay South Asian boy for marriage. Platonic relationship only." I got many hits. There were John and Pradeep and several others. We tried. We "dated." We talked. My plan was always clearer and more urgent than theirs. I had thought of all the details. They had general interest. They wanted to alleviate their shame. I wanted to alleviate my mother's pain. We all wanted to save ourselves. We didn't stay friends.

By twenty-five the pressure to marry was explosive. Every phone call, every visit, and every interaction was riddled with my mother's fury at my refusal to consent to an arrangement. She would look for anomalies in my flesh, in my words, in my breath. Her death was imminent. God would not bless me. I had hurt my parents irreparably already. My social justice work meant nothing. How could it if you made your mother die? I rolled my eyes, but I believed her.

By that time, my partner was the roommate who was conspicuously omnipresent in my life. She was the girl my mother came to suspect, hate, and (we hoped) like despite herself. I was desperate, and we needed a plan. We prayed for a gay husband we could live with and perhaps grow to love. We could play make-believe and find happiness. We would create a new kind of family, an intentional family, of three. If he had a partner, it would be four. We would have children and live in a home with a secret back stairwell where we could change living arrangements when we had parental visitors. My parents would grow fond of my partner. They would never fully understand, but would come to know her and love her as family. We would make a Bollywood film of our life story. We would all have love, and no one would die. We would find freedom by the time I was thirty. This was the plan. I set it in stone. There was no room for error.

We prayed to the gods and goddesses for a man who would bring us simplicity and peace, and not leaving much to chance but thinking we were, we found him. We found a kind-hearted gay boy who wanted community, love, and family.

There were rules attendant to this plan. My mother knew them always. I knew them sometimes. My girl didn't know them very often. I would get mad when she got them wrong because if things went wrong, I would fall apart, we would fall apart, and I would have to go home. My parents would take me away from everything we hoped to build. Still, I pretended we had open hearts, family, peace, and love. I played make-believe so much that we believed our own fairytales. We had spiritual commitments to save the un-savable and do the impossible. We would live to tell the tale Bollywood-style with smiles and happy endings. There were no cracks. There couldn't be. We were falling apart at the seams from inside out. But we didn't know that yet. We were the bits of color in something lifeless, and we would toe the line and remain, faithfully, full of life.

Zero

I married a man in January 2007. We came back home to Boston where we had purchased a "marital home," the condo around the corner from where my partner and I lived. I would not live there except when my parents would visit, but the plan was for the three of us to inhabit both places as much as we could. This would be the beginning of our intentional family. We needed to believe we were choosing this. My partner and I decorated and furnished this home, hoping the process of putting pieces of ourselves into this creation would bring us some peace. We filled that home with the brightest of colors.

One ceremony, extended family acquiescence, and three receptions later, my mother's continued rage towards me was palpable and inexplicable. She did not remember how to smile or laugh. She did not grow warm with the light I thought she had lost long ago and that my wedding should have reinstated in her. Weekend visits were just as painful, my mother cruel and demanding with inexplicable sadness in her eyes. She would still die on account of me because of the shame I had caused her. She said she felt alienated by me and was repulsed by my choices. I remembered a card I had written to her once several years back. I had written, "Mom, each day that passes, I am struck by how much more I am like you as you are like me." She looked into my eyes for what felt like the first time. With love. With satisfaction. My mother didn't want me anywhere but with her. The three of us were looking for the reward of peace and freedom we had promised ourselves we would see. It wasn't happening. If anything, it felt worse.

The thing about parceling yourself into a hundred pieces is that it wears on you. I wanted it to hurt less. I Googled "queer feminist spiritual therapist" looking for healing. I found one on the first try. That was over four years ago. I went to her seeking less pain and learned quickly that there's no quick fix to a heart that has broken in many places.

She was unwaveringly patient, kind, and compassionate as she bore witness to my pain. I remembered how to cry again – to feel again. I don't know if it's possible to express the depth of my gratitude and love for this woman who I will always hold in my heart as the person who has shown me the love, fierce protection, and wisdom that a parent can offer and that a child deserves. She brought me to life.

With her, I started to give words to what a small part of me has always known was true. I was emotionally, physically, and sexually abused by my mother. She wanted a partner, not a daughter – and one she could control into submission with cruel words and violence. My father stood by and let that happen. It was I who was betrayed. I was robbed of the love and protection a parent should provide. I looked as well at myself, as I had been living, honestly and clearly for the first time. I had built a world that could not be sustained without damage. I had to take accountability for the pain I had caused my partner when her world became so small alongside my own. I had to face the pain I would cause as I unraveled a world I had promised to a kind-hearted gay boy with whom we traveled far and long. I saw that you can't hold on to love that hard or force color and light into places that are painful and necessarily dark. We had built houses of cards, and they needed to fall. I needed to let them fall.

On April 17, 2008, I wrote my parents a letter telling them clearly and affirmatively that I was gay. I wrote to them of how much I loved them, of my desperation over the past several years, and of my longing for their happiness and acceptance. I prayed they would see me as I am. I prayed they would see me as I always have been. But they saw me as they always had.

I got hate mail for several months stating in the most graphic terms exactly what I was and exactly how I would suffer and die for causing my mother such pain. Then came the manipulation. Then came the silence. Now and again, there are attempts to contact me but always so clearly driven by the narrow and unrelenting desire to have me back by my mother's side at any cost. I don't know if we will ever have contact in the future. I do know that there is no going back.

Six

I have had to learn that I will never have the mom I want. I will never have an *Amma*. And sadly, I won't have a dad either since he's so utterly entangled in her world. I forget these lessons sometimes when watching other parents with their children or on Mother's Day, or those mornings when you wake up cold or sick or overtired. Those days, I long for an Amma more than God herself.

The tender-hearted gay boy and I are now divorced. We had promised him a communal family and then took that away. We betrayed him. He has given us the gift of allowing us to rebuild a relationship with him. He is part of our queer family.

I am continuing to walk a path of learning what our hearts really look like and feel like when they're open. The kind of open where you try not to have secrets from yourself. I am getting to know the little girl with braids and the bindi with OshKosh overalls who got lost in smoke and mirrors for so long. I am helping her grow up and grow strong.

My partner and I have survived all of this. We are mending the pieces of our hearts that were broken in this long journey and we are learning new ways of finding comfort in our own skins and voices. I married her on September 25, 2010, on our twelfth anniversary. We made vows we could promise one another, at long last, freely. And, in October 2012, we welcomed into the world our most precious daughter and son, beginning the rollercoaster ride of becoming Amma and Mama ourselves. Road trip caravans to the beach with Tupperware containers of thayir sadam (yogurt rice) and Cape Cod potato chips, here we come.

Draupadi Walks Alone at Night

SJ Sindu

For years now, since I turned twenty, my parents have been trying to marry me off. Aunties cup my chin at parties, turn my head this way and that, and say things like, "she's so fair, too bad she's short," and, "she could use a thicker head of hair, but she's pretty, so it'll balance out." My worth measured in pigments and strands. Point: I look younger than I am. Point: I'm neither skinny nor fat. Point: I come from a good caste.

Someone in a Bollywood picture says that progress is when a woman decked in gold can walk alone down the street at night. Of course a film version of civility would include 22-karat bangles and jumka earrings. In the movie, a woman tries it. Police freak out. Comedy ensues. Centuries of feminine rage unspool on celluloid.

This is a rage we've all inherited, folded up in the pleats of cotton sarees, transmuted from the heads of our mothers at the same time they scolded us for not knowing how to cook daal, and how will we keep a man happy? We learn our anger through osmosis, or maybe it's in the breast milk, spreading through our veins long before we learn how to look only at the floor and walk without showing our ankles.

In rural India, women are still married off to their rapists, a practice considered both a punishment for the rapist and justice for the woman.

My own insides curdle with this anger. I cut off my hair, hoping the outrage will seep out through my scalp, but it lingers.

In the Mahabharata, Draupadi marries five brothers and bears their children, rules as queen and eventually ends up suffering in exile. For all that, she is called a whore. A queen, and for all that, a man can still gamble her away, a man can still drag her out to the middle of a crowd and order her stripped, a man can still save her body from shame.

Every time I go back home, my mother tells me what to pack. *Bring shorts, but not too short, mid-thigh to knee, and for gods' sake make sure you bought them from the women's section. If you bring men's tank tops, I swear I will burn them all.* My mother has a problem with androgyny.

By the time I'm twenty, I identify as a lesbian. I've cut my hair. I've bought twice as many men's tank tops. And the boy I bring home to my mother still has the girl body he was born with. My little brother, who is eight, is not confused. My mother cries. My father is stone.

Draupadi spends the first year of her marriage with the oldest brother, the second year with the second oldest, and so on. This so that everyone will know which son belongs to which father. She is the lynchpin of the story, a victim of masculine sexuality like Sita of the Ramayana. The narrative revolves around her, but unlike Sita, no parents today name their daughters Draupadi. Why is Sita the virgin and Draupadi the whore? Why am I the pariah if I refuse to swallow my rage?

The questions are simple. But no one asks them. No one wants answers. No one even wants the questions. The questions are landfills that loom like mountains.

I tell my mother I'm bisexual. Bi, from the Latin *dui*, the Greek *di*, the Sanskrit *dvi*. Meaning double. Having two. Living in two. I have bifurcated: my life, brown and white; my family, my parents and me; my body, masculine and feminine. Bi, meaning two. Draupadi the wife and the whore. Bi, meaning co-existence, meaning contradiction, meaning war.

I spend years meeting potential suitors who are arranged by my parents. I don't think they'll work out, but I want to keep my parents from the breaking point. My mother calls to say that I'm not trying hard enough, and why can't I just be a good daughter and make them happy?

One suitor asks me to cook for him, watches me as I make curried beets, assures me that he can handle the spice I dump in. He can't.

Later, in a bar, a drunk white man asks us when we are getting married. *You both have good teeth*, he says, *and you're both from the Hindu Kush, so why wouldn't you marry each other?* Because I like women. Because my white boyfriend is holding empty my space in his bed, wondering when I'll come home. I can tell the drunk man that I will marry this suitor and make my parents happy, but that would be a lie.

Before Draupadi is a mother, she is a wife, and before she is a wife, she is a daughter, begotten through prayer from the fire god Agni. A princess so otherworldly that only a man who can shoot a fish in the eye can have her. But she is still a woman, and so she is an object, a prize to be won and a prize to be shared.

As I near thirty, my parents grow more desperate. They consult astrologists, cross-check with priests and mystics expert in past lives. They learn that I was a landowner named Indrani who treated her workers poorly and was doomed to pay for it in the next life. She didn't allow her female workers to take time off to be with their husbands, and so my married life will be rocky.

My mother prays for me, fasts for me, chants the Lord's 108 names every day for me. She says the chanting is supposed to help with her own anger, too. All I can tell is that my rebellion has numbed her, and I've inherited her anger.

Some say Draupadi got what was coming to her because she had insulted kings and scoffed at their bids for her hand. She laughed at one king when he fell, *the blind son of blind parents*, she had said. Of another king, she had said, *I will not marry a man of mixed caste*. So they called her a whore. They wanted her bared naked in front of her court. They wanted her fallen. And still some say they loved her.

You're going to end up alone, my mother tells me. *It's because of your anger. Your anger pushes men away.*

When Draupadi's mother-in-law mistakenly orders her sons to share the prize they've won, Draupadi becomes angry and tries to leave. What if she *had* left? Would she have married a different man and been happy? Would she have been queen? Would we know her name?

I come out to my mother three times. Each time she consoles me, sits by me while I cry, strokes my hair and tells me that I can still marry a man and have children, that I don't have to be different if I don't want to. Bi, meaning two paths. One path lets me stay in their lives. The other sees me cast out. My mother tells me to choose.

Lord Krishna explains to Draupadi that in her past life, she asked for a husband with five qualities. And since no perfect man exists, she got five husbands. In the end it is all still her fault, and still not her choice. In the end, she gets no choices. In the end, she swallows her anger, marries the men and becomes a devoted wife, which my mother would say is a good choice.

At my cousin's wedding, everyone tells me I'm next. *The stars are lining up*, they say. *You'll be married within the year*, they say. No one seems to be worried that I'm still single. They're hoping the next suitor will work out.

At a coffee shop after the bar, I tell the next suitor about my bisexuality, my polyamory, my plans to not have children. He blinks, sips at his latte, avoids eye contact. *You didn't have to tell me that*, he says. *You could have hidden that from me. You'll have to hide it from everyone if we get married.* I drink my coffee to keep the anger down.

My therapist is worried about my health. *Have you had suicidal ideation? This world needs you.* My boyfriend is tiring of my anger. This rage sits between us, grates against our skins like sand pressed too hard. I contemplate being alone. If Draupadi had given in to her anger and walked away, would she have died alone? Is that the kind of story my mother would use to scare me into obedience?

Progress – like a woman's worth – is not measured in gold. It's not measured in gossip, eyelashes, or honor. Progress is the ways in which our gendered roles have blended and blurred. My mother went to grad school. My father cooks some nights. My brother grew up in day care. But my mother says that we've had enough. She says, *further progress will unravel us.*

Draupadi, I want to rewrite your story. I want you to walk away. I want you to get fist-clenchingly, world-shakingly mad. I want your rage to cut through everything and spin the world into new string. I want to use that string to bind my mother's idea of progress to mine, to weave my own rage into an armor against assumptions and expectations, to wrap up tired old gender ideas and burn them in effigy. Draupadi, I want to inherit your anger and use your string to stitch my two selves back together.

Cut

Natasha Singh

It was my brother, Ravi, who found the switchblade in a patch of grass and gave it to me. But it was a flawed finding, for the tip was broken off. "What am I supposed to do with this?" I asked him.

Giving me a pained look, he shifted uncomfortably. "It's for protection," he mumbled, his cheeks reddening. Turning from me, he quickly rubbed his eye. As I stared at the knife uncertainly, he offered a reassuring smile. "Don't worry," he said. "I'll fix it for you," as if that was the reason for my hesitation. Sure enough, the next day he took it to the woodshop at school and got one of the nerdy boys to fix it for me good as new. I kept it with me at all times. After a few weeks, the weight of it made holes in my coat pockets, and then it slipped through one of the holes and lay in the lining of my coat like a comfortable stone, a reminder that I finally had protection if I needed it.

Having that switchblade was like carrying a loaded gun. It gave me a sense of power and invincibility even though I didn't know the first thing about using it. At school I rarely took it out, and if I did it was never in front of my teachers. Instead, I waited until recess for my brother to find me. If anyone attempted to bully him that day, I searched for that person and shoved him hard against the brick wall of our school. "If you come near my brother again," I'd whisper menacingly, pressing my knife against his throat, "I'll cut you. Do you hear me?" Looking back, I suppose I was acting out a part I wished someone would play for me.

With my switchblade, dark lipstick, and newly shaved head, I was a one-woman gang. I believed that power came from intimidation, from making others know fear as I did. I believed it came from taking over bodies – from occupying them like we do landscapes – with the intent to obliterate all that is magical, wild, and free. Without recognizing it, I had adopted the language of my father, the dominant language of the world. I walked down the hallways and smiled to myself as students made wide arcs around me. In my classes, I took to sitting in the back row with my legs sprawled out as if I were indifferent to learning. I mouthed off to my teachers and got suspended time and time again. "We don't know what's happened to you," my teachers began saying, shaking their heads in teacherly disappointment. "You used to be such an obedient girl." I couldn't tell them that within a year my father had changed just as dramatically as me; that as soon as I'd become a woman in his eyes, he'd begun beating me for staying out, for acting shamefully, for threatening to lose my honor

Regardless of his rages, I loved him fiercely and instead hated the arrival of womanhood with all her curves and her peculiar musky scent. Additionally, having a father who perpetually looked old made it harder to reconcile his violence with his age – even harder to reconcile the need to protect myself with the need to protect him. After each beating, he almost never failed to press my palm against his one eye. "I'm so sorry," he would weep into my hand just as he had when I was a child. As I'd gaze into his glass eye, it would occur to me that his vision reduced me to half – that he might never see me whole. "Forgive me," he'd plead. "I'll never do it again." Years later, when I found myself with a man prone to violence, I would discover how well trained I'd been.

But once I got my knife, I began to hope I could carve out a passage for myself, maybe slice a hole inside my dreaming and slip through, never to return. Maybe I believed I could wield it in the air like a magical wand, that the heavens would see me as a Durga Ma without a tiger, a young Goddess in the making. But if I had all of those fantasies, they came to nothing. Or perhaps that's not entirely true, for on the night I finally dared pull that knife on my father, I did cut through time, through the cord that bound me to him.

৵

I was fourteen and on my first date with a boy in my sister's grade. Greek, and possibly the only boy in our school who had a moustache, he reminded me of Victor Newman from *The Young and the Restless*. Each time he smiled in my direction I grew nervous and hoped he would whisk me away somewhere – pluck me from my life.

I walked around town with him (though it felt more like dancing), talking and trying my best to flirt as I'd seen the other girls in my class do. I laughed loudly at all his jokes and even attempted some of my own, hoping he would be won over, that he would find me different – beautiful. In an alleyway, just behind the pizza place where most of the kids in town hung out, he stopped, turned to me expectantly, and we kissed. It was a long passionate kiss, and I remember thinking, *Finally!* As he walked me home, our palms shyly touching, I wanted to dance with joy, to shout out: *Someone actually likes me!*

My parents must have sensed something was amiss, for when we neared my house, I saw my father waiting at the window, his head a dark spot against the brightly lit kitchen. As soon as he saw us, he rushed down the front steps, my mother not far behind him. Pulling on his shirt, she kept pleading with him in Hindi, "Come back! Please don't do this." But she was no match for his anger.

"Don't you touch my underaged daughter," my father screamed, shaking his fist in the air. "She belongs to me! I will kill you, you bloody monster!" Hindi curse words streamed out of his mouth, so awful they made me flinch. In the distance, my parents resembled fighting shadows as my mother kept tugging on my father's shirt, even as he shook her off. Faces gathered at windows – our neighbors' shocked eyes taking in the spectacle of my parents, of us. "Why are you doing this to our family?" my mother moaned in my direction. "Why can't you ever listen?" I had no answer for her and stood frozen with guilt. "You have become a dirty girl. Staining our family name." It began slowly, softly at first – a steady stream of Hindi words for slut and prostitute began to flow out of her mouth – a polluted river I would later drown in when I was alone.

Hot tears of embarrassment stung my eyes as I looked up at the boy who had walked me home. But he wouldn't meet my gaze. Instead, he turned on his heel and walked briskly in the other direction. I watched his back before turning to walk heavily into the house. As I passed by my father, I stopped and whispered, "I hate you."

Minutes later, he burst into my room where I was sitting on my bed, my head in my hands. "What did you say to me?"

Looking up, I took it all in: that wild look in his eye, his hands clenched into fists. My mother whimpering somewhere behind him. Without thinking, my hand slipped inside my pocket and my fingers closed around it. Pulling the switchblade from my pocket, I clicked. In the silence between us, it made a snapping sound like teeth. Brandishing it like a sword, I approached my father. "Don't come near me anymore," I began. "Just get out of my room." But the threat had nothing to stand on, not even the thin edge of a newly sharpened knife.

Snatching the knife out of my hands, my father flung me hard against the wall. "This is not your room," he reminded me. "Everything is mine, do you hear me?" My body hit the door first and then the wall before I slumped forward. Looking up at him in a dazed sort of way, my mouth betrayed me by tipping into a crooked smile. "How dare you laugh at me?" he shouted. I made myself stand up then, my knees strangely wobbly like tender reeds in the river.

Pushing me onto the bed, his hands squeezed around my neck, pressing down, pressing in. "I'm going to kill you," he panted. "You are thankless dirty whore." It was then that I heard the screams of my mother or maybe I imagined them. Maybe it was just me trying to scream through the loss of air, through the terror. I remember his eye bulging; my entire world was reflected there, and I knew that if my father pressed harder, it would burst. I think it was then that I first slipped out of my body, and it seemed to me that I was no longer afraid – just floating. Crouched over air, I placed a hand over my heart and watched.

Years later I'd recall this moment when training to be an advocate for survivors of domestic violence. Our guest speaker, a kind-looking police officer, had come to discuss responses to 911 calls. In the middle of his talk, a woman in the class raised her hand and shared how she'd once called the cops because her husband had tried to choke her. The police officer paused as if considering his words, "We no longer use the word, 'choking,' Ma'am. He was strangling you, so we consider that attempted homicide." Shaken, I would duck my head and try to quell the panic that had risen up in me like a startled bird. By then my father would be an old man – a changed man – and our relationship would be tender and sweet. Filled with a quiet sort of peace. It's true that over the years my family would seldom speak of the brutal violence that took place. If the subject arose, both my parents would insist that I provoked those beatings, leaving me turning in circles even as I loved them.

Releasing his grip on my throat, my father grabbed hold of my head and began slamming it against the dresser drawers, my desk, the dresser again and again. The sharp corners, I was convinced, had pierced my skin, my skull. I don't know how long it lasted, the deep cracking sounds, the sounds of women wailing all merging together. Then there was silence.

As if in slow motion, I slipped from his hands and stumbled to the window. "Somebody help me," I called out. In the distance, near the creek that ran thin and fast near our house, a lone female figure looked up and around as if unsure where the screams were coming from, as if unsure they were coming from anywhere at all. I wanted to swoop down on her arm like a bird; I wanted to become a fish and follow the watery trail of the creek. Then my father's hand was pressing on the back of my head again, pressing my face, my tongue against the screen until all I could taste was blood and metal. "This is what a hook must taste like," I thought before things grew fuzzy. I knew, without knowing, that I'd been caught.

Sometimes I feel like I'm still trapped there against the window, above my childhood bed, clawing at feeling, my own body, at memory itself. "I'm stuck," I say to my husband who tells me, "Write about it until you can cry." Funny, he can weep over these stories, over this time in my life, while I can't. I envy him, his capacity to feel deeply for the girl I once was. I want to tell him that it is dangerous, this mining of memory. That to write to bone is to push into a chaos so bad it robs me of knowing that I have feet, am still standing. That I am now a woman who can put down this pen and walk away.

For weeks after that night, I could no longer hear loud sounds or voices, even laughter, without flinching, without wanting to sink to the ground and curl up into a ball. Even now, I can barely tolerate loud sounds – the clattering of dishes, shrill laughter, a certain pitch of voice. "Shhh," I often say to others when their sounds penetrate my world; and when they look at me quizzically, I will smile, pretending it's the schoolmarm in me. "I'm sorry, but I've got an inner librarian on board," I laugh self-consciously, as if it can smooth over the tightness in my body, on my face. What I never told anyone is that for weeks and months after that night, I would rock back and forth on the floor, beating my knuckles against my head and biting my lower lip until I drew blood. And all the while I rocked like a girl on the edge of a dangerous precipice. I prayed to the Gods whom I was sure were no longer listening: *"Please Krishna, Shiva, Kali, Hanuman, Durga, Vishnu, Brahma, Lakshmi, Ganeshji, don't let me go crazy. Please save me from myself."*

After my father disappeared from my room, I was left in a quiet so thick it was as if flies had filled my ears, as if in the distance there was a murmuring crowd. It occurred to me that something different had happened – that this time my father's fury had entered my skin, my soul. It had found the opening in me and once in, had tried to break my spirit, snap my heart in two. And in that quiet, came a new thought – one I had feared but didn't want to face. *No one will protect me; no one will hear my cries. I am alone.*

I remember frantically raking my hands across my body, touching the places my father's hands had been, but I could find no way to yank out the rage he'd planted. My fingers wrapped around my throat. Where had my voice gone? I wondered. When I came to a sitting position, I heard myself make a small, soft whimpering sound. But it no longer sounded like me.

Operation Make My Family Normal

Mathangi Subramanian

It was a November afternoon in 1988, and my mother was ruining my life.

I knew it as soon as I walked through the front door, my cheeks and fingertips still pleasantly frosty from the almost-winter Wisconsin wind. The air in the house rattled with the clatter of popping mustard seeds and the sizzle of frying potatoes. My stomach grumbled at the delicious smells, but I ignored it.

Now was not the time for human weakness.

"Amma!" I yelled, kicking off my boots and shimmying out of my puffy winter coat. "What are you doing?"

"Making dinner," she said, as I barged into the kitchen. The counters were piled with chopped vegetables and plastic containers of multicolored spices. A ball of dough sat in a metal bowl by the sink. A packet of cilantro sprawled fragrantly in a corner.

It was terribly, terribly wrong.

"Do you have any idea what today is?"

"Thursday?"

"Thanksgiving!"

"Oh right. Thanksgiving," she said, holding back a smile. She dropped a handful of cashews and raisins into a pan of butter with an angry splatter.

"It's a holiday," I said. "We should be having a holiday meal. Something special."

"We *are* having something special," she said. "No sambar tonight. I'm making chapatti and fried rice."

"Not that kind of special!" I knelt down on the orange and brown tile floor, digging through the bottom cabinet until I found what I was looking for: a tin can with a blue and red label. I pulled it out with a flourish. "This kind of special."

"What's that?" my mother asked. As if she didn't know.

"Cranberry sauce," I said, banging the can on the counter. "It's what you're *supposed* to eat on Thanksgiving."

"We can have it with the chapattis," she said.

"You're not *supposed* to have it with chapattis," I said. "You're *supposed* to have it with mashed potatoes and stuffing and pumpkin pie."

"Well that's perfect, because I'm making potato curry," my mother said.

"Not potato curry," I said, my thick fringe of bangs quivering in fury. "Mashed potatoes. That's how American families do it. That's what we should be doing."

"Next you'll be wanting turkey," she said, tossing the raisins and cashews into a pot of basmati rice as though it was the most natural, appropriate thing in the world.

I stormed out of the room. Couldn't this woman see what she was doing? Eating Indian on Thanksgiving was – what was it exactly? It was uncouth, unnatural, unheard of, maybe. Definitely un-American.

In short, it was weird. And when you are eight years old, there is no bigger nightmare than being weird.

That Thanksgiving marked the unofficial beginning of Operation Make My Family Normal, also known as Mission Impossible, a quest that would carry me through the better part of the next decade.

It started at school, when we were having a discussion about pilgrims and Indians (the other kind, of course), and how great it is that the U.S. was a country of immigrants. This always made sense to me, since my own parents had come from a country that I had only been to once, before I could remember, and that existed in my head mostly as a blur of mosquitoes and sweat and tropical flowers.

But this year, I started to notice something. Throughout history, people were divided into right and wrong. There were the right kind of British, who came to America on a ship looking for religious freedom, and the wrong kind of British, who wanted to tax tea. There were the right kind of pioneers, who respected the land, and the wrong kind of pioneers, who destroyed it. And of course, there were the right kind of immigrants, and the wrong kind of immigrants.

We were the wrong kind.

We didn't have ancestors who came to American on boats in petticoats and buckled hats. We didn't have names that were shortened on Ellis Island. We didn't eat meat or go to church. We didn't have grandparents in Lacoste or flannel pajamas or cupboards full of sunblock for the beach.

As for the few American things we did do – well, we did them all wrong. I showed up to piano recitals in mirror-work skirts instead of lacy dresses; during dinners at friends' houses, I struggled with silverware after a lifetime of eating with my hands.

In third grade, I came to two realizations: First, something had to change. Second – and most importantly – I was the only person in my family savvy enough to do it.

It seemed to me that my family's inability – or, as I saw it, unwillingness – to correctly celebrate American holidays was the easiest to fix. If we could make a few annual changes, I decided, not only would I be spared the humiliation of pre- and post-holiday assignments like "What I did for Thanksgiving" and "How I Celebrate Christmas," I would also be able to share my classmates' anticipation of events in the months leading up to the holiday in question – all evidence that we were rapidly transitioning from wrong to right and, most importantly, from weird to normal.

I pictured an end to silences during discussions of shopping expeditions for Easter dresses or musings about the contents of the next pocket on the Advent calendar. Instead, I would be an active but nonchalant contributor, off-handedly remarking on the traditions my family had clearly been keeping for generations – or, at least, for this generation.

Most of the holidays were beyond repair. Easter, for example. Although the Easter bunny did make an annual visit to our house, it wasn't enough to sustain a conversation in the third grade cafeteria. As for Christmas, forget about it – too many decorations, dishes, and details for novices like us to tackle.

But Thanksgiving? That was all about eating. Indians are experts at eating.

To be fair, we aren't just experts at eating – we're also experts at everything that has to do with eating: preparing food, consuming food, forcing others to consume food, packing leftover food for people to take home. Sure, I knew that vegetarians like my family wouldn't touch turkey, but there were other vegetables that we could work with – my mom was a whiz at currying beans and potatoes, for example. And although she had never attempted sweet potatoes, I was pretty sure they couldn't be too different from taro root, which was my favorite curry of all. Plus, Thanksgiving was about family – and that was something we had plenty of, even if it wasn't on this continent.

Yes, I thought, Thanksgiving was our gateway holiday. First Thanksgiving, and then the world. (Or, at least, the 50 states.) And so, the weekend before Thanksgiving, I accompanied my mother to the grocery store, where I convinced her to add a can of cranberry sauce to the cart, a can that I excavated just in time for our almost-Desi dinner.

It was the little things, I told myself, that could save us all from death-by-weirdness.

As my mother set the table for Thanksgiving dinner, I opened the can of cranberry sauce and divided it four ways, plopping the day-glo, gelatinous portions onto each of the metal dinner plates we used every night.

"What's this?" my brother asked. He scrunched up his nose and poked at the shivering mass.

"Cranberry sauce," I said perkily. "It's a traditional Thanksgiving dish."

"It looks like ectoplasm."

Sensing an opportunity, I nodded vigorously. "It's a lot like ectoplasm."

"But ectoplasm's green."

"It can be red too."

"Daddy, can ectoplasm be red?"

We turned just in time to witness my father tipping his cranberry sauce onto my mother's plate.

"Dad!" I cried.

"Honey, have a bite," my mother said to my father.

"How?" he asked.

He had a point. We always ate with our hands, and the cranberry sauce defied our usual scooping techniques. All four of us looked from the sauce to each other and back to the sauce, unsure how to proceed.

"I'll get a spoon?" my mother finally asked. She got up to get some silverware.

"You're not supposed to *eat* ectoplasm," my brother said, sticking out his tongue.

Deciding it was time to model some good behavior, I helped myself to a chapatti, and used a warm, soft corner of it to scoop up a piece of cranberry sauce. I shoved it into my mouth with a smile on my face. The cranberry sauce tasted sweet and sour and slippery and downright disgusting. The chapatti was delicious.

Which was, of course, the problem. Being Indian wasn't just easier than being American. It was better. Being Indian was warm, mouthwatering, comfortable. It was knowing what to do and what to say – maybe not all of the time, but more of the time than being American. It wasn't canned and stuck on a grocery store shelf for everyone to purchase. It was mine. Nobody else's but mine.

But at that moment, when I was surrounded by friends and teachers and TV shows that were telling me that I wasn't enough; when my family had no idea what it was like to be the only brown girl for miles around; when I was desperately trying to figure out who I was before I had no friends and no confidence; at that moment, I thought that canned was the answer. Just open and pour, like everyone else. Even if it was hard, and bitter, and a little bit gross, it seemed like the way out.

And so I did what I had to do. I took another bite.

My brother stared at me intently, obviously wondering if I was about to die.

"Scrumptious," I lied.

By that time my mother had returned with a spoon. She put a bit of the sauce on my father's plate before she cut herself a sliver. She held it in her mouth for a minute, swallowed, and gagged.

"Oh," she said.

We stared at her in silence.

"I don't think it really goes with curry," said my father, who still hadn't tried any.

"Well if you don't want yours, I'll have it," I said, holding out my plate.

My mother, possibly also picturing my canned-monstrosity-induced-death, got up again and said, "Let's save it, shall we? And you can have it later."

"Like how Americans eat Thanksgiving leftovers all week," my father said.

My mother reappeared with a Tupperware container that she began to fill with the rejected red goo.

"I'll have mine for leftovers," I said loudly. "Maybe for lunch when we go back to school."

"Of course," she said, sealing the lid and putting it on the counter behind her.

As much as I hated to admit it, my parents were right. This American holiday thing was not as perfect as I thought it would be.

When we returned to school on Monday, for the first time ever, I couldn't wait for my teacher to ask the inevitable question.

"How was your Thanksgiving?" she finally said.

My hand shot up in the air.

"Yes, Mathu?"

"It was great!" I said, beaming. "We had cranberry sauce and…um… potatoes."

"What about turkey?" a girl behind me asked.

"She's vegetarian, remember?" someone else called out. The whole class laughed.

"Now, now, everyone. Remember, differences are what make our community richer," my teacher said. She smiled at me, but she was as blonde and turkey-stuffed as everyone else in the room. I sank lower in my chair, wishing I had kept my mouth shut. "Tell us, Mathu. Did you eat with your family?"

"Yes," I whispered, hoping to avoid the unavoidable next question.

"Who did you eat with? Your grandma? Your grandpa? Aunts and Uncles maybe?"

I shook my head, and said, "My parents and my little brother." I was too mortified to launch into my usual explanation of how my relatives all lived in India, and had decided long ago that three flights and a twelve-hour layover in a German airport full of Uzi-toting guards was hardly worth a four day holiday.

"Oh," my teacher shook her head and clicked her teeth. "Just a little affair, huh?"

My friend Jennifer had immigrated to the United States from England two years before. She nudged me and whispered, "Don't worry. My grandparents didn't come either."

Clearing her throat, my teacher asked, "Jennifer, do you have something you want to share with the class?"

"I was just telling Mathu how good our turkey was," Jennifer said. "My mom makes the best cranberry sauce in the world."

Who were these people, and where do they come from? I wondered, silently adding "taste buds" to the list of things about me that would never measure up.

"Mmm," my teacher smiled and nodded approvingly. "You know, there's really nothing more American than some good, old-fashioned cranberry sauce."

Later on in the cafeteria, everyone opened their lunch boxes and let out a collective groan.

"Turkey sandwiches," Katherine moaned, "and cranberry sauce."

"The same thing we had all weekend," Adam said, nodding dolefully.

"Leftovers," Jessica groaned.

"What do you have for lunch, Mathu?" Jennifer asked me.

The truth was, I didn't know – and I wasn't sure I wanted to know. There was a real possibility that my mother could've kept her word and packed me left over cranberry sauce, like we discussed at dinner. That meant that I could join the conversation and officially be normal.

But it also meant I would have to actually *eat* the cranberry sauce.

Well, I said to myself, this is what it takes to be American, right? So let's do this.

I undid the plastic clasps of my bright red Care Bears lunch box and took a deep breath which, quickly, became a sigh of relief. Inside was my favorite lunch: a row of tightly rolled chapattis stuffed with potato and beans curry, neatly lined up in a Tupperware box. Not a drop of cranberry sauce in sight. Only weirdness. Delicious, homemade weirdness.

"Leftovers," I said, trying to sound tragic. But it was probably hard to hear me with all that chili and cumin and cilantro in my mouth.

Normal would be easier if it didn't taste so terrible.

Contributor Biographies

Tanzila "Taz" Ahmed is an activist, storyteller, and politico based in Los Angeles. An electoral organizer by trade, she's mobilized thousands of Asian American & Pacific Islanders to the polls in over seventeen different languages in the past fifteen years at various non-profit organizations, starting with founding South Asian American Voting Youth in 2004. She is cohost of The #GoodMuslimBadMuslim Podcast that has been featured in *O Magazine*, *Wired*, and *Buzzfeed*. An avid essayist, she had a monthly column called Radical Love, was a blogger for *Sepia Mutiny*, has written for *Truthout*, *The Aerogram*, *The Nation*, *Left Turn Magazine*, and more. She is published in the poetry collection *Coiled Serpent* (Tia Chucha 2016) and was published in the anthology *Love, InshAllah: The Secret Love Lives of American Muslim Women* (Soft Skull 2012). Her third poetry chapbook, *Emdash and Ellipses*, was published in early 2016. Taz curates Desi music at Mishthi Music where she co-produced *Beats for Bangladesh* and she annually makes #MuslimVDay Cards. Her artwork was featured in the shows *Sharia Revoiced* (2015), in Smithsonian Asian Pacific American Center's "H-1B" (2015), and *Rebel Legacy: Activist Art from South Asian California* (2014). You can find her rant on twitter @tazzystar and at tazzystar.blogspot.com.

Jabeen Akhtar was born in London and immigrated with her Pakistani parents and three older siblings to the United States when she was two years old. She is the author of the novel *Welcome to Americastan* (Penguin/Viking,

2011) and is a contributor to the *Los Angeles Review of Books*. Follow her on Twitter at @jabeen_akhtar or visit her website at www.jabeenakhtar.com.

Roksana Badruddoja is a feminine-masculine woman, a Bangladeshi American, a Buddhist Muslim, a queer mother to a fierce 13-year-old girl, and an Associate Professor of Sociology and Coordinator of Women and Gender Studies at Manhattan College. Dr. Badruddoja's research in the areas of race and ethnicity, sexuality, gender, religion, and culture, and how these impact South Asian-American women has, been published in numerous peer-reviewed journals. These include the *National Women's Studies Association Journal*, the *International Journal of Sociology of the Family*, and the *International Review of Modern Sociology*. She is the author of *Eyes of a Storm: The Voices of South Asian-American Women* and the editor of *New Maternalisms: Tales of Motherwork (Dislodging the Unthinkable)*.

Neelanjana Banerjee's writing has appeared in *Prairie Schooner, PANK Magazine, World Literature Today, The Literary Review, Asian Pacific American Journal*, and more. She is co-editor of the award-winning *Indivisible: An Anthology of Contemporary South Asian American Poetry* (University of Arkansas Press, 2010). Based in Los Angeles, she is the Managing Editor of Kaya Press and teaches fiction for Writing Workshops Los Angeles.

Piyali Bhattacharya is a writer, editor, and writing instructor based in Nashville, TN where she is Writer-in-Residence at Vanderbilt University. Her work has appeared in *Ploughshares, The New York Times, The Wall Street Journal, National Geographic*, and many others. She is the editor of the anthology *Good Girls Marry Doctors: South Asian American Daughters on Obedience and Rebellion*, which was awarded a grant from the National Endowment for the Arts. She holds an MFA in Fiction from the University of Wisconsin - Madison, and is currently working on her first novel, an excerpt from which won the 2015 Peter Straub Award for Fiction. She can be reached at www.piyalibhattacharya.com.

Madiha Bhatti is a South Asian American daughter who drinks three cups of chai a day. She graduated from the University of North Carolina at Chapel Hill with an English major and women's studies minor. She is returning to her alma mater for medical school, to the delight of her parents and the dismay of South Asian cliches. She's spent the past two years alternately teaching in Thailand and working towards a master's degree in religious studies. She is a spoken word artist, community activist, and unabashed morning person. Her greatest rebellion to date is owning a motorcycle but no one ever believes she did it.

Meghna Chandra is an organizer and writer. She graduated from the University of Pennsylvania with a BA in urban studies and "went back" to India for her MA in modern history from Jawaharlal Nehru University. You can find her biking around Philadelphia, marching against injustice, reading and writing radical science fiction, and becoming a part of lovingly critical communities wherever she goes.

An entertainment journalist who's written for publications from *The New York Times* to *Cosmopolitan*, **Sona Charaipotra** is the co-founder of CAKE Literary, a boutique book development company with a decidedly diverse bent. When she's not hanging out with her writer husband and two chatter-boxy kids, she can be found poking plot holes in teen shows like *Pretty Little Liars* – for work, of course. Sona is the co-author of the YA dance drama *Tiny Pretty Things*. She's been adapting her screenplay *-30-* into a novel for more than a decade. Find her on the web at SonaCharaipotra.com, or on Twitter @sona_c.

Originally trained in pediatrics and public health, physician and writer **Sayantani DasGupta** teaches in the Master's Program in Narrative Medicine, the Center for Race and Ethnicity, and the Institute for Comparative Literature and Society, all at Columbia University. She also co-chairs the Columbia University Seminar on Narrative, Health and Social Justice. She is widely published and anthologized and writes about race, gender, stories, and health online and off. She's the proud mom of a good boy and good girl who can become doctors if they want to. Learn more about her work at: www.sayantanidasgupta.com.

Tara Dorabji is a writer, strategist at Youth Speaks, mother, and radio journalist at KPFA. Her work is published or forthcoming in *Al Jazeera*, *Tayo Literary Magazine*, *Huizache*, *Good Girls Marry Doctors*, Center for Asian American Media, *Mutha* and *Midwifery Today*. Tara is working on novels set in Kashmir and Livermore. Her projects can be viewed at dorabji.com.

Bangladeshi-American poet, editor, and educator **Tarfia Faizullah** was born in 1980 in Brooklyn, NY and raised in west Texas. She received an MFA in poetry from Virginia Commonwealth University and is the author of *Seam* (SIU 2014), which US Poet Laureate Natasha Trethewey calls "beautiful and necessary," as well as *Register of Eliminated Villages* (Graywolf 2017). Tarfia's honors and awards include a Great Lake College Association New Writers Awards, a Pushcart Prize, a Fulbright Fellowship, a Ploughshares Cohen Award, a Dorothy Sargent Rosenberg Prize, as well as scholarships and fellowships from Kundiman, Bread Loaf, Kenyon Review, Sewanee, and Vermont Studio Center. Her poems appear in *Poetry Magazine, Poetry Daily, Oxford American, Ploughshares, jubilat, Kenyon Review, New England Review*, and elsewhere. More at: www.tfaizullah.com.

Triveni Gandhi recently completed her PhD in political science at Cornell University. Her research interests include gender and issues of economic justice in the US and abroad. She currently lives in New York where she works on state-wide political issues.

Rajpreet Heir lives near Washington, DC, and is a third-year in George Mason University's MFA program, where she is the sole recipient of the 2015-2016 Nonfiction Thesis Fellowship. She is Indian British American and writes about growing up in Indiana.

Leila Khan lives and works in the Bay Area. Her writing has appeared in two other collections: *Love InshAllah: The Secret Love Lives of Muslim American Women* (Soft Skull 2012), and *Beyond Belief: The Secret Lives of Women in Extreme Religion* (Seal Press 2013), which was considered by the *Washington Post* as one of the Top 50 Nonfiction Books in 2014. She was born in Pakistan and lived in various countries in Asia and Europe before settling in the US Her favorite places in the world are Strasbourg, Dubrovnik, and Maui.

Rachna Khatau is an actress, singer, and TV host. Among her many TV, film, and stage credits, Rachna recurs as Sondra on *Baby Daddy* (ABC Family) and was signed to a 2012 talent holding deal with ABC. An improviser and sketch comedian, Rachna has performed her two-woman show, *MR. (with the period),* to sold-out crowds in LA, Chicago, and Austin. She was signed to a record deal with a subsidiary label of Universal Records, has hosted over eighty live TV shows, and worked as a red carpet correspondent for *Extra*. Rachna has a master's degree in Broadcast Journalism from the University of Southern California. Born in London and raised in Chicago, Rachna now lives with her husband in LA More at www.RachnaKhatau.com.

Swati Khurana was born in India, and lives and works in New York City. Her art has been featured at Brooklyn, Bronx, and Queens Museums, and DUMBO Arts Festival (NYC); Chatterjee&Lal (Mumbai); Museo de Arte y Diseño Contemporáneo (Costa Rica); Scala Mata Gallery (53rd Venice Biennial); and Zacheta National Gallery (Warsaw). Her collaborative project "Unsuitable Girls" with Anjali Bhargava was in the Smithsonian's "Beyond Bollywood" exhibition. Her writing has appeared in *The New York Times, Narrative.ly, Asian American Literary Review,* and *Columbia Review.* She has received grants from the Jerome Foundation & Bronx Arts Council, and was a founding member of SAWCC (South Asian Women's Creative Collective). A Kundiman fellow, Swati is working on her first novel, tentatively titled "The No.1 Printshop of Lahore."

Surya Kundu was born near Kolkata, India in 1987. She moved to the Bay Area in 1990 and discovered a lifetime of people mispronouncing her Bengali name (the Y is secretly a J.) She graduated from Amherst College in 2009 with a BA in anthropology and then received her law degree from the University of Michigan Law School in 2015. She is currently a litigator in Washington, DC While not at work, Surya's obsessions include petting every puppy, eating her way around the world, intersectional feminism, and reconciling her proletarian politics with her weakness for bedazzled sweaters.

Ayesha Mattu is an American writer and editor. Her groundbreaking anthologies – *Love, InshAllah: The Secret Love Lives of American Muslim Women* (Soft Skull 2012) and *Salaam, Love: American Muslim Men on Love, Sex, & Intimacy* (Beacon 2014) – have been featured globally by media including the *New York Times,* NPR, the BBC, the *Washington Post,* the *Guardian, Times of India, Dawn* Pakistan, and *Jakarta Post.* She was selected a 'Muslim Leader of Tomorrow' by the UN Alliance of Civilizations, and has served on the boards of IDEX, the Women's Funding Network, and World Pulse. Ayesha is an alumna of VONA/Voices writers' workshop and a member of The Grotto.

Fawzia Mirza, actor, writer, producer, is a 2015 Chicago 3Arts Awardee in Acting, was named a "Top 10 Creative" by *Indiewire Magazine,* and was named a 2016 Whitehouse Champion of Change in Asian American Art and Pacific Islander Art and Storytelling. Legendary actor Zia Mohyeddin said of Mirza, "Some actors hold an audience, a few possess it. Some actors light up a scene, a few ignite it...Mirza belongs to the latter category." Mirza believes in dispelling the myth of the 'model minority' in mainstream media and in the power of comedy to tackle divisive topics. Her one-woman play, *Me, My Mom & Sharmila*, explores her relationship with her mother through their shared love for Bollywood heroine, Sharmila Tagore, has performed at universities, conferences, and festivals across the country, and has toured internationally, including a three-city tour in Pakistan. Mirza has produced, written, or starred in web series', short films, documentaries, and plays. Her first feature film, *Signature Move*, about a Pakistani Muslim woman seeking her identity in love and wrestling, releases in 2017.

Nayomi Munaweera is a Sri Lankan-American writer. Her debut novel, *Island of a Thousand Mirrors* (Hachette India 2013), was long-listed for the Man Asia Literary Prize and the Dublin IMPAC Prize. It was short-listed for the DSC Prize for South Asian Literature and the Northern California Book Prize. It won the Commonwealth Regional Prize for Asia. *The Huffington Post* raved, "Munaweera's prose is visceral and indelible, devastatingly beautiful – reminiscent of the glorious writings of Louise Erdrich, Amy Tan, and Alice Walker, who also find ways to truth-tell through fiction." *The New York Times Book Review* called the novel, "incandescent." The book was the Target Book Club selection for January 2016. Nayomi's second novel, *What Lies Between Us* (St. Martin's Press), was hailed as one of the most exciting literary releases of 2016 from venues ranging from *Buzzfeed* to *Elle* magazine. Her non-fiction and short fiction are also widely published. www.nayomimunaweera.com.

Jyothi Natarajan is an editor and writer based in Brooklyn. She is managing editor at the Asian American Writers' Workshop, where she runs *The Margins*, an online arts and ideas journal. She fell for journalism working at *The Caravan* magazine in New Delhi, and is a longtime board member of *IndyKids*, a social justice-oriented newspaper written for kids, by kids. She hopes one day to make almond butter in her Vitamix.

Phiroozeh Petigara is a Pakistani-Canadian writer and educator who has found her home in Oakland. As she moves away from the clutches of being a Good Girl and works her way towards being a Real Woman, she finds her life blooming with unimagined beauty. She currently teaches older adults to tell their life stories on an interactive online platform, as well as Bollywood Fitness to South Asian older adults, and yoga to incarcerated and returning citizens with the Prison Yoga Project. Her writing world has expanded from novels to personal essays, flash fiction, and anything else that strikes her fancy. She has curated readings as part of the Bloom Series and has been published in the *Karachi Literature Festival Anthology*. She writes sporadically on phiroozeh.blogspot.com.

Ankita Rao is an American journalist currently based in India, where she writes about health, education, and inequality for publications like *The New York Times*, *The Atlantic*, *Slate* and *Quartz*. Ankita is originally from Tampa, Florida and attended the University of Florida, where she studied journalism, religion, and creative writing. She is also an alumna of the Columbia University Graduate School of Journalism.

Hema Sarang-Sieminski can be found in and around Jamaica Plain, MA with her wife and three kids, and their furry babies Sophia and Dorothy. She finds food for her soul in the roots of trees, in watching nature through her children's eyes, and in the quest to stay open-hearted to all that life brings. By day, she is an immigration attorney in private practice in Jamaica Plain, MA. She has advocated on behalf of survivors of violence for over fifteen years and brings to her work a commitment to the hearts and spirits of all of us on the margins.

SJ Sindu's debut novel, *Marriage of a Thousand Lies*, is forthcoming in 2017 from Soho Press. She has received scholarships from the Lambda Literary Retreat, the New York State Summer Writers Institute, and the Nebraska Summer Writers Conference. Her creative writing has appeared or is forthcoming in *Brevity*, *The Normal School*, *The Los Angeles Review of Books*, *apt*, *Vinyl Poetry*, *PRISM International*, *VIDA*, *Black Girl Dangerous*, and elsewhere.

Natasha Singh's work has appeared in the Modern Love Column of the *New York Times*, *Threepenny Review*, *Crab Orchard Review*, *South Asian Review*, and in several anthologies. She is a two-time recipient of The Canada Council Grant for her creative nonfiction. Alongside teaching workshops on sex ed in the age of porn culture, she serves as Co-Chair of the board at the Center for Domestic Peace, a nonprofit dedicated to ending domestic violence, and is Executive Director at Asha Rising, an organization devoted to creating safe housing for elderly women who have aged out of the sex industry in Kolkata, India. Natasha currently resides in Oakland.

Mathangi Subramanian is the award winning author of three books for children and young adults. Her work has appeared in publications like *Al*

Jazeera America, Quartz, The Hindu, The New Indian Express, Gender and Education, Hunger Mountain, and the anthology *Click: When We Knew We Were Feminists* (Seal Press 2010), among others. In 2016, her novel *Dear Mrs. Naidu* (Zubaan 2014) was shortlisted for the Hindu Goodbooks Fiction Award, and in 2015 her story *Banu the Builder* was the middle grades category winner of the Katherine Paterson Prize. A former public school teacher, assistant vice president at Sesame Workshop, senior policy analyst at the New York City Council, and Fulbright-Nehru Senior Scholar, she received her doctorate in communications and education from Columbia University Teachers College in 2010. Her husband is not a doctor, but she thinks he's pretty great anyway.

Aunt Lute Books is a multicultural women's press that has been committed to publishing high quality, culturally diverse literature since 1982. In 1990, the Aunt Lute Foundation was formed as a non-profit corporation to publish and distribute books that reflect the complex truths of women's lives and to present voices that are underrepresented in mainstream publishing. We seek work that explores the of the very different histories from which we come, and the possibilities for personal and social change.

You may buy books from our website or by phoning in a credit card order.

www.auntlute.com

Aunt Lute Books
P.O. Box 410687
San Francisco, CA 94141
415.826.1300
books@auntlute.com

This book would not have been possible without the kind contributions of the Aunt Lute Founding Friends:

Anonymous Donor	Diana Harris
Anonymous Donor	Phoebe Robins Hunter
Rusty Barcelo	Diane Mosbacher, M.D., Ph.D.
Marian Bremer	Sara Paretsky
Marta Drury	William Preston, Jr.
Diane Goldstein	Elise Rymer Turner